DAUGHTERS
of
NAZARETH

Hope you enjoy.
Love
Eileen,

DAUGHTERS *of* NAZARETH

*A remarkable story of loss,
hope and discovery*

PATRICIA HUGHES

MACMILLAN
Pan Macmillan Australia

Many names in this book have been changed to protect privacy.

First published 2002 in Macmillan by Pan Macmillan Australia Pty Limited
St Martins Tower, 31 Market Street, Sydney

Reprinted 2002 (twice)

National Library of Australia
Cataloguing-in-Publication Data:

Hughes, Patricia, 1955-.
Daughters of Nazareth.

ISBN 0 7329 1121 4.

1. Hughes, Patricia, 1955–. 2. Nazareth House (Brisbane, Qld.). 3. Orphans – Queensland
– Brisbane – Biography. 4. Church work with orphans – Queensland – Brisbane. 5. Foster
home care – Queensland – Brisbane. 6. Adult child abuse victims – New South
Wales – Sydney – Biography. I. Title

305.906945092

Typeset in 12.5/15 pt Bembo by Post Pre-press Group
Printed in Australia by McPherson's Printing Group

For Sandra.

I feel blessed and grateful for every day I've known you. My world is by far a better place because of you and the happiness you've brought me.

For David.

For your love, patience, understanding, strength and for believing in me. You are my light in the darkness, the fire in my heart, my anchor and my life.

For Mark and Tony.

For all the years of happiness you've given me and for just being you.

Contents

CHAPTER 1

---✛---

Conjuring up the Images

There are moments which mark your life. Moments when you realise nothing will ever be the same and time is divided into two parts: before and after. Sometimes you can see these moments coming but sometimes not; and, as with me, they hit you when you least expect them.

My moment was February 27th 1997.

At forty-one, I was a single mum holding down a full-time job and raising two teenage boys, a big enough job on its own, while maintaining a house and the chores that go with it. Like a lot of other women.

It was only days until autumn and unseasonably hot, so I'd taken advantage of Thursday's 'late night shopping' where I could at least be in air-conditioning. The shops were packed with customers and the aisles were jammed with trolleys. I pushed mine around impatiently, dodging the slower shoppers like a racing car driver.

My whole day had been a rush, from 5 a.m. when I'd risen to go to work through to my brief arrival home at 4.30 p.m. to put dirty clothes in the washing machine and prepare dinner before hurrying out to do my grocery shopping.

1

With the boot of my car full of food, I pulled up into the driveway, stepped out and ran my fingers through my shoulder-length blond hair. I glanced at the long grass and the garden full of weeds. This was a sad time of year for my garden. The gardenias, wattle and agapanthus had already bloomed and the dead flowers hung forlornly on the end of stalks. But the weeds were very happy.

I enjoyed the solitude of gardening but there just never seemed to be enough time to get around to it, what with school meetings, basketball games and personal crises for each of my two boys. Something always came up that was more important, and all too often it became difficult enough just to juggle my free time between them.

I opened the boot, took out two bags of groceries and walked towards the front door. Asleep on the mat, as usual, was my seal-point Persian cat, Oscar. Stepping over him, I muttered, 'Don't get up, Oscar. I know you must be exhausted. Please don't disturb yourself.' He recognised my voice and twitched an ear but still lay comatose on the doorstep.

Lazing in the lounge room, one on each couch, were my two teenage boys. Their eyes and their smiles gave me a moment's attention but I knew their brains were still absorbed by the sitcom on the television. They were good friends despite the difference in age. Mark, the eldest, was seventeen and Tony was fourteen, and even though they had the inevitable squabbles, they remained loyal and protective of each other.

Through my tiredness, a feeling of pride surfaced as I watched them. The unselfconscious happiness I was witnessing was what I'd been working for during the past ten years. It had been a long struggle after my divorce but I had been determined that I would make our new life work for us.

I had often thought that by now I'd have my life in good shape. I'd be a wife, mother and a businesswoman. I'd serve my customers by day, study and help my children by night, find time for the basketball games and snuggle up to my husband as each day ended. In fact, the only part of my life I was completely happy about was the children. *That*, I reassured myself, *that* I had done right. There was no way I would let their lives be affected by the break-up of my marriage the way mine had been affected after my own parents' relationship had disintegrated. Their break-up, when I was seven years old, had been the beginning of a life I would never allow my children to endure.

As I walked into the kitchen, I called out to Mark to bring the rest of the shopping in from the car and ten minutes later I had placed the last of the grocery items haphazardly in the pantry, thanking God the day was nearly over.

Tiredness washed over me again as I walked to the bathroom to splash cool water on my face. As I glanced in the mirror, I noticed that dark circles were etched in the soft skin under the muddy green eyes that gazed back at me. I had always tried to take care of myself. I exercised regularly, never smoked, rarely drank and watched what I ate. Now I couldn't remember ever feeling more tired.

But now, having started thinking back on my youth, I didn't have the resistance to stop my mind from conjuring up the images of the past. The memories of those early days are disjointed but, in the end, horrifying to me.

CHAPTER 2

(1959)

✥

Peg Dolls and String Bags

Happiness for me at four years old was skipping the three kilometres to the local swimming pool on a hot summer's day with a towel around my neck and one shilling in my pocket. I was alone and oblivious to any peril as I skipped back again at dusk, more often than not to an empty flat.

When I look back on my childhood, it amazes me that I didn't become a statistic, a small child abducted, raped or, worse still, left for dead by the side of a quiet road. There certainly were a few characters that looked capable of doing such a thing. We lived in Spring Hill, Fortitude Valley, which is in the heart of Brisbane yet on the fringe of the central business district. People came there—and still do—with little or no income. They could live on a pension, pay affordable rent and survive on a shoestring budget. What was typical of these low-income areas was the large number of bars and pubs dotted around, to which everyone gravitated as their only means of entertainment and escape. Even though money was inevitably in short supply, spare cash could always be found for a round of drinks with friends at the pub. It was a place where both men and women retreated to keep warm in winter and to cool down in the summer.

In Brisbane, winter brought clear blue skies and bitter westerly winds that howled relentlessly through the cracks of walls and cut like a knife through every layer of clothing. Summer brought beautiful hot, humid days and the inevitable afternoon thunderstorm. This rainy season seemed to shorten the days, making the early evenings just plain murky, with the flickering streetlights doing very little to brighten the dismal streets.

Although Fortitude Valley had its occasional beauty, it also had a forlorn feeling about it, with a hint of hopelessness. But it was where I lived. It never occurred to me to be astonished that so many riches could exist in the city centre only three streets from the abject poverty of my neighbourhood.

It's said that the most important years of a person's life are the ones before the age of five. These early experiences build character and shape personality. They made me self-reliant and independent far beyond my years.

I wonder what other people would have made of me at age five, and what possible future they would have predicted.

My mother, Merle Rose Mooney, carried inside her all the legends and superstitions of the Irish, a part of her that I have inherited, much to the consternation and amusement of my friends. She was a pretty dark-haired woman whose ancestors were born in Cookstown, Ireland, before immigrating to New York in the early 1800s like many other Irish. Times were very hard and—again like so many—they came to Australia, 'the land of opportunity', where jobs were supposed to be plentiful.

Memories of my mother from this time are very fragmented. My main impression is that she was absent a lot of the time. In my mind's eye I see her at the hairdressing salon, obviously a big occasion for her, while I sat on the doorstep with a Matchbox car in my hand, or walking to and from my school with her until a suitable bus route was found.

Every Sunday, we would walk to St Stephens for Mass. I guess you could say I was a Catholic of sorts. When you're young, you don't appreciate all the pomp and ceremony. I just liked the bobbing up and down.

I do remember one day towards the end of my first school year, when I wore home a party hat that I had just won in a game of 'Simon Says'. I practically slept in it, until eventually it broke, causing torrents of tears. This must have really pulled at my mother's heartstrings because I remember her desperately trying to fix it, even though by then it was destined for the bin.

I spent most afternoons after school playing outdoors for hours, only running inside at sunset and coming to a startled halt at the sight of my mother, hands on hips, legs slightly apart, looking down at me. Her heart-shaped face always seemed to be creased in a frown, her lips pressed tightly together. I remember looking up at her and noticing her dark hair always permed and set in place, her dress always clean. She had a full figure, green eyes and a fair complexion; sometimes sallow from too many hours spent indoors.

I remember once she said to me, 'Just look at yourself!' At five years old, I took this statement literally and glanced over to the full-length mirror on the wardrobe. I saw myself: a tiny child, still with that little-girl chubbiness, no front teeth and my fine sandy hair hanging untidily in my eyes. My overlarge dress was filthy from hours spent on the dusty footpaths while cars drove past belching smoke from their exhausts and dust from their tyres. I looked down at my shoeless feet and saw tiny toes that resembled black jellybeans. I must have scraped my shin at some time during the day because a small trail of blood had run down one of my bandy legs and dried in the shape of a dead worm. At the time, I had no idea what she was talking about. I looked no different than I did most days.

Another memory that stands out in my mind is my mother's warning, 'Beware of strangers. Some of them are devils in disguise.' Up until then, I'd had no fear of strangers as I wandered the streets, but from that point on, before I spoke to a person I always looked for a tail sticking out behind them. I never did see one. Though memories of my mother are few, I didn't choose to forget things about her—she just wasn't around enough for me to remember much.

My father, Ernest Joseph Gourgaud, on the other hand, is forever turning up in so many memories and was the one constant in my life. He was a handsome Frenchman with almost black hair and large, deep-set cornflower-blue eyes that seemed to shine when he smiled. He appeared very tall to me as I looked up at him. A giant. His voice was a quiet rumble that could have been the result of too many cigarettes; his nicotine-stained fingers always seemed to have a cigarette in them.

He could trace his ancestors back to General Gourgaud, Napoleon Bonaparte's private physician and one of the people with Napoleon on the island of St Helena at the time of his death. General Gourgaud was subsequently the prime suspect in the poisoning since he was the doctor. Obviously, the fall of France led to a slight decline in fortunes for the Gourgaud family as well.

My father was an uneducated man and this, without doubt, led to a tough life which eventually saw him enlisting to fight in the Second World War in the famous 9th Division of the Australian Army. He served as one of the 'Rats of Tobruk' in North Africa, and later helped repel the Japanese advance in New Guinea.

To some, the 9th Division heralded fame in battle, but to others it spelt death or disablement. Dad saw it all as an orderly with the medical corps, collecting the dead and injured near the front lines and bringing them back for care, or identification and burial. It was during his time in the military that he contracted tuberculosis (TB) and was shipped back home, where he subsequently had one of his lungs removed. The loss of his lung gave him a slightly lopsided appearance, with the concave area of his back quite obvious. His condition had him in and out of hospital regularly, as the remaining lung had been damaged considerably as well. His heavy smoking couldn't have helped.

Many times I would accompany him, patiently waiting in the X-ray Department of Greenslopes Repatriation Hospital (at that time a hospital for ex-servicemen and women and their families) for our names to be called. Even though I never felt unwell, it was always both of us who had our chests X-rayed, standing in long green gowns with our chests pressed firmly against the cold metal plate while the technician told us to, 'Breathe in. Hold it. Okay. Breathe out.' This seemed to happen every few months for no reason whatsoever and Dad always made a game of it, treating it like an outing.

I remember sitting on the grassy slope outside Ward 12/13 of Greenslopes playing with the toads that were in abundance (the very thought sends shivers down my spine now). I was oblivious to the incapacity my father lived with, while my mother sat inside with him.

I always associated Dad with colours. When he was around, my life was a golden colour but when he was in hospital, it was a dull grey. He was a kind and gentle man who never so much as raised his voice to me as far as I can recall, although like any child I probably deserved it at some time or other. He had other ways of chastisement that left more of an impression than any physical punishment.

There was one time when, on my way to the swimming pool, the sight of a beautiful doll in a shop window caused me to forget all about my planned swim. I ran back home to ask if I could have the doll, as any five year old would do. A handful of wooden clothes pegs that I'd painted smiling faces on were the closest thing I had to dolls, and this doll dressed in a flowing wedding dress had all the physical attributes my peg family didn't have. I instantly and desperately wanted it.

Finding no-one at home, but seeing Mum's purse in the kitchen, I searched through it to find the ten-shilling note that matched the price tag I had seen. Not even thinking about how I would pass this new addition off at home, I raced back to the shop only to find that someone else had bought the doll in the meantime.

Too dejected to continue on to the swimming pool, I returned home, only to find Dad in the kitchen fully aware of the missing money. The disappointment in his eyes sent a knife through my heart. As he knelt down to look straight at me, he asked quietly, 'Why did you do it?'

This question was all the punishment that I needed. I realised that I hadn't measured up to his ideal of me and that my taking the money was something he hadn't expected. I knew I'd let him down, and no spanking was required as I silently vowed never to do anything like that again. I realise now just how much money was involved in this act of petty larceny. It must have been divine providence that the doll had already been sold so that I never had the opportunity to spend what must have been a large part of their week's wages.

I also discovered that Dad had a subtle sense of humour. One day while walking back from visiting my mother's brother Terry, we saw a woman with flaming red hair, and I commented on how beautiful it was. In reply to my asking what colour her hair was, he told me that it was called 'strawberry blonde'.

'What's mine?' I asked.

'Honey blonde,' he replied.

I looked up at him and asked him what colour his hair was.

'Mine is chocolate blonde,' he said as he smiled and winked. Dad seemed to have answers for all those tough questions five year olds have.

My parents' relationship was most likely doomed from the start, probably due to the fact that my father was already married with three children when he met my mother and had been refused a divorce by his Catholic wife. I'm sure this would have caused my mother to feel very insecure. These must have been tempestuous times for my parents and Mum would disappear for lengths of time, perhaps looking for that security. But despite all the separations, she always came back to Dad.

The combination of my wonderfully French father with his carefree passion and humour together with my fiery Gaelic mother was the perfect recipe for a life, if not harmonious and smooth, then certainly interesting and unpredictable. Each of them had Celtic ancestors and were therefore dramatic, as well as romantic, people. Celts have often been dreamers who looked beyond the daily cycle of drudgery to a world of infinite possibilities. The outward expression of this resilient optimism was a love of beautiful things, as well as music and stories in which men were strong and brave, but were enthralled by women whose passions defied convention.

I can see that with such a heritage, my parents may have been drawn to each other with passion forsaking reason. While caught up in a relationship that they couldn't live without, they would also have found it increasingly difficult to live with. Did they love each other? Did I even know what love was at that age? It was simply something the nuns at school told me about.

As I write this account of my life, I remember in my later teens having a compulsion to make my parents live in front of my eyes again, to bring them out of the shadows and have them play their parts for me. I wanted to see where things went wrong, where the threads of our lives started to unravel. I wanted them both to be as clear to me as two photographs might be. Of course, that never happened.

I suppose my parents needed each other and that could be called a love of sorts. I can only surmise that like so many people both then and now, in defiance of their families and finding themselves in a socially frowned-upon relationship, they gravitated to the city in search of some degree of anonymity.

Home for us in 'the Valley' was a small flat consisting of two rooms, the largest being a bedroom with an unused brick fireplace at one end, concealed by two wooden doors that opened from the centre outwards. This old fireplace served as a storage cupboard for us and housed our summer clothes in winter and our winter clothes in summer. My parents' bed and mine were on opposite sides of a narrow walkway that led away from the fireplace, with a small wardrobe that held our meagre selection of clothes at the base of my bed, and a bench seat that was our lounge at the foot of theirs. There was no radio, no drapes and no carpet on the cold linoleum floor.

On the other side of a curtain that separated the two rooms was a ramshackle kitchen containing a table, three chairs and an old icebox. I would crouch out of sight behind this curtain once a week, watching a huge man with a bald head and black curly hair on his back and shoulders fill our doorway while carrying a large block of ice in a pair of vicious-looking callipers, placing it with ease in the top of our icebox. He had seemed like someone out of a Brothers Grimm story full of witches and trolls and hulking woodsmen.

Another curtain partitioned off a tiny alcove that contained a toilet and a bath. I remember sitting in the bath at night, asking why our soap had no smell and why it was 'scratchy'.

Visitors were rare at our home. A few of the other old tenants in our block sometimes showed up smelling of stale beer, sweat and cigarettes. On one occasion, an old, gnarled man with a gappy smile, a scrawny neck and unkempt grey hair that stood out like a halo around his head tried to have me sit on his lap.

He was probably no more than fifty, but his five o'clock shadow, red eyes and haggard appearance made him look a lot older. When he whispered that I should take my knickers off first, my father unceremoniously threw him out. Although the reason for the old man's request was never fully explained to me at the time, I put it down to the fact that I had been playing outside in the dirt and my knickers must have been so dirty that he didn't want his own clothes dirty as well.

Sadly, his was the sort of request I was to hear too many times in later years.

Our occasional visitors were the same men who would sit on the wooden bench in our courtyard, surrounded on three sides by flats, looking through the clothes hanging on the clothesline at other residents walking by. It wasn't unusual to see them sitting on their doorsteps in the shade on hot, sticky summer days with temperatures up in the thirties, wearing only their underpants in an attempt to keep cool; a glass of beer in one hand and a newspaper in the other, brushing flies away from their faces. The smell of trash, piled high in unemptied bins, lingered strongly in the humid air and ensured there were plenty of flies to keep them busy.

Another visitor was our fat landlord, Mr Conlon, always dressed in a black suit and tie like an undertaker, with his thinning hair greased over his balding head. Compared with our neighbours and the way they dressed, he seemed akin to an actor in costume. Every week he would come over and pat me on the head while waiting for the rent money. After he left, my mother would say, 'He's such a snob. Nobody wears full suits any more.' The first time I heard her say this I hunched my shoulders and covered my mouth with my hand, trying to stifle my uncontrollable giggles. Not knowing what I was laughing at, my mother and father both looked at me with raised eyebrows and quizzical looks. I was actually imagining fat Mr Conlon collecting the rent in his underpants, minus his suit and looking just like all the other old men who were our neighbours.

Always an occasion to look forward to was a visit from Pop, Dad's father. This statuesque white-haired man, invariably well dressed and wearing a hat, would cross his legs and sit me in the hollow of his upturned foot, bouncing me up and down while holding onto both of my hands. Other times, he would walk around the room with both my feet on top of his, my hands caught in his hands, while I giggled delightedly. He could make coins disappear magically from his hands and make them reappear from behind my ears. My mother never smiled much when he was around and she would always make an excuse to go somewhere else soon after he arrived.

I thought my life was pretty normal—not having any basis for comparison—even though the dominant emotion of my early years was loneliness. With Mum at work at nights and Dad visiting the hospital, the horseraces and the pub on weekends, I had a lot of spare time to spend alone. What an amazingly undisciplined world existed for me as I walked around the neighbourhood finding my own fun and entertaining myself, making friends with anyone who would talk to me, as long as there was no tail poking out of their coats. My favourite pastime was to sit outside our flat in the gutter with my basket of wooden clothes pegs, playing 'families' with them, imagining them to be the brothers and sisters I didn't have.

I loved walking barefoot in these same gutters on rainy nights when I had been sent to the local shop for bread and milk. I would splash and kick my legs through the flooding water, coming back totally drenched, with the milk (glass bottles in those days) carried in an old string bag, and sometimes minus the change that had fallen out of my pockets while I skipped back home.

Going to the corner shop was a challenge in itself as a five year old when one of the streets to be crossed was St Paul's Terrace, a busy street even by today's standards. There were no traffic lights, so waiting for a break between cars was the only means of crossing to the other side of the road.

Once I had successfully crossed a few times, bringing the change home was the next obstacle to overcome. The loose change was sorely needed in our home and, after the first few losses, steps had to be taken to ensure its safe arrival. I couldn't be trusted simply to walk now that I had learnt how to skip, so my mother would lay out one of my father's large handkerchiefs on the table, place the money in the centre, collect all four corners together and tie them in a knot. This process was repeated by the shopkeeper with the change, and the handkerchief was placed in the bag with the milk for me to take home.

Foolproof—or so everyone thought.

My newfound success in returning with the change obviously went to my head and these trips to the shop became an anticipated outing. My exuberance was expressed by a gradual increase in skipping, jumping and swinging of arms now that the change was 'unloseable'.

Unfortunately, on one fateful night I started swinging the bag and its contents of milk bottles in high circles, angled from ground level to above my head and back again so it turned like a ferris wheel.

I soon discovered the laws of physics through practical application. A misplaced skip in the middle of my swinging ended the game abruptly when the inevitable happened: both bottles smashed together above my head, saturating me with milk.

This couldn't have happened in a worse place than outside the local electrical store where people were crowded around the front window watching the flickering blue lights of the televisions that were still a novelty in 1960, and a totally unaffordable luxury for all our neighbours. I'm sure that most adults with children have seen something similar in their own children's lives and as such would have regarded me with amusement and understanding. However, to me it felt like the whole world was witnessing my embarrassment as I stood dripping on the footpath, dreading the reception I knew would be waiting for me at home.

On my return, I sheepishly presented the bag full of broken glass to my mother, only to be given a bath in stony silence after an exasperated look. I was then dispatched straight back to the shop again, for a final attempt at getting two bottles of milk back to the house intact. This incident was never repeated; the look on my mother's face as she held the bag of broken glass was enough to curdle the milk.

But at least I'd brought the change back!

The old string bag that I used to carry home the milk served more than one purpose for me. At this time, my hair was an unruly mess, cut fairly short because of its straightness and fineness, and always on my face and in my eyes. But I yearned for long hair that I could tie back in a ponytail. Regularly, I would secure the plastic handles of the bag on top of my head with bobby pins while the crisscrossed strings fell down my back in a blue cascade as I pretended I had my longed-for tresses. The sight of me sitting in the gutter, laughing and talking to my handful of pegs with this blue string bag on top of my head, never failed to bring smiles to the faces of passers-by.

If I wasn't playing in the gutters, I was wandering the streets alone and barefooted, sometimes poking my head into a shop, smiling and waving, saying, 'Hello'. It was a sparkling world, full of adventure and promise.

On our street, next to the electrical store, was a newsagent where I would stand and flick through the pages of comics on display before the shop owner came over saying, 'Off with you, then. Go on, off with you.'

Next, there was a post office where pictures of beautiful stamps covered the walls. There were always people coming and going so I never lingered long. After that, there was a bakery where the lovely smell of fresh bread wafted out at me as I smiled and waved. Sometimes the shop owner would call me in and give me the broken legs or arms from the gingerbread men before shooing me away gently as if I were a straying hen.

I was well known to most of the shop owners by the time I was six years old and most of them would reply to my greeting with a 'Hello Trish' as I made my way up the road to the Alliance Hotel where I knew Dad would be. I can still almost smell the sour aroma of beer coming out.

After seeing me standing in the doorway, he would call me over, produce a handkerchief and spit in it to make it moist enough to wipe some of the dirt off my face and hands, before buying me a drink. This hotel where my father would sit and talk to his friend Larry was the meeting place for most of our neighbours and was situated on the opposite side of the road from the corner shop.

Larry, a very timid, quiet man with an almost submissive manner, had a large, disfiguring strawberry birthmark that started at the hairline above his left eye and extended downward over his cheek, ending just above his chin. Although he always lowered his eyes and stared at his beer glass whenever anyone passed by, he would sit and talk quietly to my father for hours. While they both consumed glass after glass of beer I swung my feet on a high stool, eating chips and drinking 'double sarsaparillas', made from a mixture of sarsaparilla cordial and sarsaparilla soft drink. Although I cannot recall Larry so much as saying a word to me, Dad would often look over at me, wink and smile, and then continue with his conversation, leaning forward slightly to hear Larry's quiet voice. I adored my father with his clear blue eyes, and wished that my eyes were like his instead of the same muddy green as my mother's.

The hotel was only a couple of streets away from our flat. It was just a short walk to Nanna Mooney's house as well. Nanna Mooney was my mother's mother and seemed to be an unfriendly woman who frowned a lot and reserved what emotion she had for my father—giving him withering looks, no doubt to emphasise her disapproval of the situation he had put her daughter in. Visiting Nanna Mooney would lead to endless visits to the bathroom to wash my hands—almost unheard of for me—just to smell her 'Cashmere Bouquet' soap.

Nanna Mooney lived in a small cottage in Rose Street with an abundance of fishbone ferns growing in front of her white picket fence. The street was barely wide enough for one car to drive through, much less two-way traffic, so the few cars owned by the residents were parked on the footpaths close to the fences. I often wished Mum and Dad had a garden full of flowers and plants growing up the fences like Nanna Mooney did.

She was not very prominent in my life, choosing to ignore me in the hope that I would just go away. She never visited us at our flat. Disapproval was very evident in her every gesture.

The last time I remember seeing my grandmother, I was four and my father and I were standing hand in hand on her front doorstep as she turned away, shaking her head in a definite 'no' before closing the door on us. This preceded my first visit to Nazareth House, a home for neglected and abandoned children, as my father was once again admitted to Greenslopes Hospital for treatment. Heaven only knows where my mother was.

My memory of this visit to Nazareth House is scant to say the least. All I know is that four months later, I was back home again in time to start Grade 1 at St Stephens School.

On the several occasions that my father was admitted to the hospital, my mother's social life seemed to increase greatly. Working nights at the local cinema obviously brought her into contact with a large group of people and she would often come home late either drunk or with a gentleman, but mostly both.

Pubs were her weakness. I suppose there is a good side to drinking in pubs. A pub has regulars—people who drink away their lives with other people who drink away theirs. No-one demands anything of you in a pub. No-one is judgmental. I could see how Mum was attracted to that life.

I would sometimes wake up in the middle of the night to hear strange grunting noises from the other bed. I knew instinctively that I had to be quiet and go back to sleep, but not before I had a quick peek through the hole in my old grey blanket. This resulted in no enlightenment for a five year old, only gave rise to the unspoken question of *What's that man doing to Mummy?*

When she went to work, I was supposed to stay inside. 'I'll be back at twelve. You be asleep by then,' she would say. I soon learnt to guess the time that she was due home and always made sure I was 'asleep' in bed when she arrived—but not before I'd made myself a bread and tomato sauce sandwich, skipped across busy Boundary Street to the electrical store with the televisions piled high on top of each other, and sat on the footpath cross-legged watching program after program. I only went home when I either felt tired or thought Mum would arrive home soon.

One Christmas Eve, the last one I remember spending at home, the electrical store owner arranged for a man to dress as Santa Claus and be in the store waiting for all the neighbour-hood children who had been invited. I arrived wearing all my Christmas presents: a beautiful pink party dress, black patent leather shoes, and a pink bow in my hair, tidy for once. I felt like a princess and at the age of six I was deliriously happy; I had everything I could possibly want.

All the children stood around with eyes agog, looking at a huge table decorated with tinsel and laden with chips, cakes and lollies. In a far corner stood a real Christmas tree dressed with baubles and flickering coloured lights. After sitting on Santa's lap and receiving a small present each, we were let loose on the table in what seemed like a feeding frenzy. We gorged ourselves and at the end of the night we went home feeling sick but happy.

It was the best Christmas I had ever had.

In the middle of my second year at school, one week after my first communion and three days before my birthday in May, my father went back into the hospital and I awoke to the sound of silence at home.

There was no noise of rattling plates coming from the kitchen or any smell of tea and toast wafting through to me. I don't remember feeling upset or worried in any way so I think waking up with no-one there must have been a regular occurrence. I had no idea what time it was but I did know it was a school day—I vaguely remember that the day before had been sports day, Wednesday.

I knew that if I didn't go to school without a good reason, I would get the cane, like I had yesterday for whistling. The year before when I had been in Grade 1, I regularly hid underneath the four steps leading up to our front door that overlooked the main road, knowing that no-one could see me. The result was that I missed the school bus and stayed there all day pretending to be at school. I had my lunch and my pegs, what else did I need? But I knew I couldn't do that this time—I could almost feel the cane on my hand from the day before.

I jumped out of bed and made my way to the kitchen, passing the pile of dirty clothes in the corner. I had to wear the clothes I'd worn the day before but that hadn't bothered me. I'd only worn them for half the day; I'd worn my sports clothes all afternoon.

I put my homework in my bag, made a jam sandwich for lunch and sat on the end of my bed eating another one for breakfast while I looked out of the window and waited for the electrical store to open. That meant it was 8.30 a.m. and there was a half hour to go before school started.

With bag in hand, I crossed the main road and started walking to school since there was no money for the bus, feeling very proud that I'd done it all by myself.

It was that afternoon, after lunch, that I found myself in the back of a police car on the way back to Nazareth House, minus my party dress and peg family, and with only the clothes I was standing up in.

I never saw my mother again.

CHAPTER 3

✤

Black Dogs

I arrived in the full splendour of any seven year old after a car ride; my hair askew and melted ice cream that I'd been given by the policemen liberally spread over me and the back seat of the police car. I felt very pleased with myself for missing most of the school afternoon but was unsure why I had been collected by two policemen when I could easily have walked home. But home wasn't where I was going.

It seemed like an endless journey until I heard the policeman saying, 'Here we are,' and sure enough, there it was again, perched on top of a hill high above Wynnum, overlooking the other old convict station of St Helena in Moreton Bay. Nazareth House.

This Catholic nunnery and care house for the aged and poor had been built in 1922. It was run by the Sisters of Nazareth, an order that had been founded in London in 1854. In 1926, the work for children commenced when twenty-five girls from various Nazareth Houses in England and Ireland arrived to be cared for by the Sisters. Over the ensuing years, thousands of girls were fostered and adopted after a short stay at the home.

As on my previous visit, I thought it resembled a castle with its scowling gargoyles crouched menacingly around the parapets and steeples which rose up into the clouds.

I have only vague impressions—you couldn't even call them memories—of my earlier short visit there at the age of four. The drama that must have preceded this event totally passed me by at the time. Had I blocked it out or, more likely, was I just too young to remember? I have no idea.

As we drove through the iron gates and along the vast drive-way, I looked around at the green paddocks on either side of us. On this day, there was a storm brewing and shafts of afternoon sun filtered through the clouds and highlighted Nazareth House as if a spotlight were shining on it. The glittering towers and arches were starting to catch the orange rays.

We were met at the entrance by the 'Virgin Mary', a large white stone statue that stood at the base of the stairs leading up to the double front doors. I couldn't believe how much bigger this building was compared with my school, St Stephens, in the Valley. I can close my eyes and see myself as I must have been: a tiny, awkward, dishevelled creature clutching the remains of the ice cream in my sticky hands, while gazing up at the building with my mouth open in awe.

I was by now quite used to the sight of nuns, so when one met us in the foyer, I had no nerves or fear. I was, however, unsure of why I was at Nazareth House at all. Led by the hand, I was taken to a stark office and told to sit and wait till someone came for me.

I remember I sat and looked around wondering how Mum or Dad were going to find me. The lady in the office continued working but glanced up often to smile at me, until a different nun came in carrying a bundle of clothes on one arm. Taking me firmly by the hand, she glanced down at me and said, 'Your face could do with a scrub.' Then with a 'Come, child,' we headed off down a long marble corridor.

Now I was starting to get scared. Now I was beginning to remember!

There was the picture of Jesus on the wall in the corridor, with his heart exposed and a crown of thorns around his head. His eyes followed me everywhere I went, making me feel that no matter what I did, I would always be observed. The clatter and clanging of kitchen utensils in the scullery directly opposite the office was layered on top of the sound of children.

I remembered that noise!

Even though I was used to raucous kids at school and I wasn't little any more—I was a Second Grader—this noise seemed to be everywhere all at once. It echoed off the walls and the cold marble floor, and seemed to increase in volume all around me, overwhelming the pitter-patter sound of my own feet on the floor.

We made our way almost to the very end of the long hall-way then turned right, passing a set of stairs leading upwards on our left, before entering a massive room with shiny wooden floors. This room looked like it held fifty beds or more. They lined the walls on either side of a walkway, the bed ends facing each other on either side of it.

Standing at the entrance to this vast room, I heard the nun say, 'Count four beds along the left, Patricia, and that one is yours.'

We turned right and entered another room. Lockers were lined up on the left side, along the outside wall of the dormitory.

'Count four again, Patricia, and this locker is yours. Remember that.'

The bundle of clothes and shoes were put in the locker, my hand was again taken and off we went once more. We made our way steadily towards the source of the noise, passing another large room on the right that could only have been the bathroom. Glancing in as we passed, I saw four baths. Four baths in one room! On the opposite wall from the baths were cubicles that contained toilets and along the walls were basins. I couldn't believe the size of this room!

Then we were through the double doors and outside to the noise. 'This is the play area, Patricia.'

'Monica,' the nun called out loudly as she looked at a group of girls tossing a ball to each other. 'Come here, please.'

'Monica will look after you,' she added, before turning around and disappearing back through the doors, leaving me standing alone on the concrete surrounded by girls my own age and older.

Monica had tortoiseshell glasses with lenses that looked like the bottom of Coke bottles and she blinked at me myopically. She had thick, wavy brown hair that she kept pushing behind her ears.

As I sat down on a nearby bench, I said self-consciously to Monica, 'You go and play. I want to wait here for my Mum and Dad to come and get me.'

'Your parents aren't coming, you know,' she said, as she pushed her glasses back up to the bridge of her nose. 'We all thought that at first but no-one ever comes.'

'Mine will,' I confidently replied. *If they can find me*, I thought, a little less confidently.

She shrugged and ran off with the group of girls, leaving me to sit and look around at my new surroundings.

Leaning back against the wall of what appeared to be the dining room, I looked over at a concrete area about the size of two basketball courts filled with girls aged from about five to twelve years old. Everyone seemed happy enough, bouncing balls against a wall or jumping rope—just like at school. I sat and watched for what seemed like hours, until a bell, rung by a nun, broke this reverie.

Monica ran over to me. 'Come on, it's dinnertime. You can sit next to me.'

We made our way into a room that contained five tables on both sides of a walkway. There were eight chairs around each table and except for two or three, every chair was filled with a noisy young girl, everyone speaking at the same time. Then, in walked a nun dressed totally in black.

Silence.

'That's Sister Philomena,' Monica leant over and whispered in my ear.

I was to find out that hell hath no fury like a 160-pound Irish Catholic nun! Sister Philomena's formidable presence was as powerful as a physical blow. Her hands were hidden inside her overlarge sleeves; her black rosary beads jangled around her waist and fell against the skirt of her voluminous black habit. The only skin visible was that on her face. Her ample bosom rose and fell as she looked around the room, and as she pursed her mouth, I noticed fine dark hair on her upper lip. With her back ramrod straight and her head held high, her eyes had the power to silence the whole room in an imperious manner that would have done Caesar proud.

Not a word was spoken by her or us.

Dinner rattled up the corridor on a meal trolley, and was served without delay. My first night's dinner was pale mince in watery gravy, mashed potatoes and peas with bread and butter, all eaten in relative silence. This tasted better than a gourmet meal to me as my last few meals at home had been self-made with whatever was available in the cupboard to put on a slice of bread. And eaten alone.

After dinner, we were mainly left to our own devices, with some girls reading and some playing in the recreation room. I resumed my vigil in the playground, feeling more uneasy and scared as time went by.

Very soon, we were all told to get our pyjamas; mine were in my locker, while the other girls collected theirs from under pillows. We were then herded off to the bathroom, forming four rows leading to the four baths, where it seemed the older girls were responsible for taking turns to wash the younger ones.

The baths were filled only once.

With our pyjamas in one hand and a towel in the other, we stood, making our way up the line towards ever cooling and dirtier water.

By watching the others as I moved up in the queue, I soon grasped the procedure. When you were at the front, you took your clothes off, ready to step in as soon as the bath was free. You washed, got out, dried off, picked up your clothes, deposited your towel in a basket near the door and went outside again.

As I stepped into the bath and sat down, an older girl soaped up a washer and scrubbed my face, ears, back, feet and hands. I was out again before I knew what had happened. It soon became obvious that it paid to be one of the first in line to have a bath because hot, clear water rapidly turned cold and grey.

Dried and dressed quickly, as the next in line would be out of the bath soon, I followed everyone else to the lockers to put our day clothes away. In my locker I discovered that I had been given three outfits, two pairs of shoes and socks and three pairs of undies—my complete wardrobe.

Bathtime completed, it now seemed to be bedtime, and everyone knelt by their bed to say prayers before pulling mosquito nets from above the bedheads, tucking them in place around the base and climbing in beneath the covers. The sheets felt clean and crisp, and the mosquito net gave my bed an eerie look as the lights were turned out and a nun's shadowy figure could be seen stalking around with a torch, doing what I assumed to be a bed check. I lay in bed with a jumble of thoughts running through my head.

Holy Dooley, am I ever going to be in trouble! Mum told me never to go outside, and to be in bed when she got home. She'll be home and I won't be! What'll I say when she eventually finds me?

If I tell Dad that the police brought me here, he won't believe me because he always said policemen were nice and that if I ever got lost, to ask one for directions and he would take me home. But I wasn't lost, I didn't ask and I'm not home!

I imagined the policemen who brought me there looking everywhere for me once they realised their mistake, starting with the office where they'd left me. I pulled back the covers and jumped up as quietly as I could. Tiptoeing out of the dormitory I came to the corridor; disorientated I turned right, stepping into a room that was at the top end of a 'T'. To my right was a long room that ran parallel to my dormitory, and to my left, through a doorway, was a classroom with two rows of desks leading away from a blackboard.

Wrong way, I thought. *Getting lost around here could be very easy—no-one else will ever be able to find me.*

I made my way back to the corridor and started heading straight towards a dim light at the other end where I could see a doorway that led outside. Totally forgetting that I was still in my pyjamas, I passed the foyer, dining room and the office. I was nearly free, nearly outside into the night, when, cutting through the silence, a voice behind me spoke my name.

'Patricia!'

I turned to see Sister Philomena standing in the hallway.

I was summoned wordlessly, her finger pointing to the ground in front of her, and meekly I obeyed.

'Where do you think you're going?' she said in her broad Irish brogue.

'Home,' I whispered.

'This is your home now,' she replied.

I had heard that statement too many times that afternoon and I'd had enough!

'I hate you and I hate it here. I want to go home!' I defiantly said to her. I must have looked like an animal ready to defend itself, and that's just how I felt.

Unmoved, she merely stared at me. There was no softness hidden behind those pursed lips. No kindness or tenderness.

Finally she replied, speaking the words slowly. 'Patricia, it's about time you realised which side your bread is buttered on.'

I looked at her blankly. *What did bread and butter have to do with anything and what did it matter what side of the bread you put the butter on?*

Taking my hand unceremoniously, she led the way down the dim corridor, past numerous doorways and several stairwells. Thank goodness she didn't just say, 'Go back to bed.' I would never have found it. Instead she led me all the way back to my bed. After pulling the covers over me, she said, 'Did you see the creatures on top of the building when you arrived this afternoon?'

I nodded, remembering the many horned gargoyles with clawed feet and wings crouching and watching me as I arrived.

'Those creatures come alive at night and turn into black dogs with long, sharp teeth and evil eyes,' she said. 'These dogs are really devils that love to eat little children and they know if you're awake or asleep. They walk around looking for hands that are hanging over the beds and they eat them! Every night, you must place your arms on your chest in the shape of the cross and the Lord will look after you and protect you and the devils will pass you by. Good night, Patricia. Stay in bed!'

My eyes must have been as big as dinner plates and with my arms crossed over my chest I watched in terror the retreating shape of Sister Philomena, too scared to move.

She wouldn't lie, would she? Not a nun!

I lay in bed that night, petrified and corpselike, barely breathing, listening for the sound of dogs' claws on the wooden floors and imagining moving shadows in every corner. I closed my eyes tightly, willing for sleep to come so I couldn't see the glowing red eyes of the devils as they prowled the corridors, their tails sticking out behind them, looking for little girls who were not yet asleep. Was this my punishment for something I'd done?

The storm had finally arrived. I could see flashes of lightning through my closed lids and I jumped at every clap of thunder.

When people say they slept like a baby, they mean that they slept well. But to me, sleeping like a baby means waking up every half hour crying. And that was how I ended my first day, listening to the water gushing down the drainpipes outside the locker room.

Sister Philomena's words were remembered many times over the next twenty years or so and the sight of a black dog would cause my heart to skip a beat every time.

CHAPTER 4

✤

Mr Pinky

After that first day in the home, weeks turned into months with very little change in routine, punctuated only by special events, holidays and treats for good behaviour. Unfortunately for me, Monica's prophecy had turned out to be right. I had come face to face with reality the same way a runaway car comes face to face with a brick wall.

Over the first few days, Monica took me on a guided tour of Nazareth. She took me up the stairs to the old people's quarters where we tiptoed arm in arm and whispered, watching them shuffling around the corridors, never lifting their feet off the floor. Down a set of stairs to an area below the main floor was the play area for the preschoolers. The kitchen, smelling like boiled cabbage, was next to this playroom and had an amazing contraption hidden in the wall called a dumbwaiter, which sent food upstairs to our scullery and on further to the old people on the top floor.

Tucked away out back of the main building past the playground was the laundry, which continually droned with the endless washing and drying that had to be done for all the children and the elderly people. Further still, down the slope past the laundry and the swings, was the nuns' cemetery.

Settling into this new way of life wasn't easy and it took me a little while. I was forever in trouble. Forever being punished. Most of the time I couldn't even understand why. I wasn't doing anything different to what I'd done back home. Why should I be punished now? In those early weeks, however innocent, I was probably seen as the organiser of any devilry that began to happen in the home. I guess I tilted at their windmills a little. My problem was I had come from absolute freedom to strict routine and discipline. Life was now structured and regimented where once it had no restrictions or rules.

Initially I rebelled, but not for long. Stamping feet and pouting lips meant nothing to the nuns. I had started my life at Nazareth by trying to fight. My independence was soon noticed and kept under strict control, giving me no choice but to accept this new life. We were expected to be docile. My fire and spirit, emotion and opinions were not acceptable. Defiance was an attitude from my past life only. It was a hard transition but I adjusted.

Eventually I became used to the home and everything that went with it. I had a bed to sleep in, the company of other children and three meals a day—most of which I had never experienced before. I was learning to co-exist. I became part of Nazareth House, learning more and more about the place they called a 'home' but which in reality bore no resemblance to one.

I remember things before I went to Nazareth House in bursts, flashes of things good and bad, but I could almost recite what happened from day to day at the home. My life was so very different from anything I had experienced before. I had to forget what I knew about living.

I was to find that routine was the basis of life at Nazareth House, with everything ruled by the clock. Each period of our day had a precise starting time and duration. Like getting up at 5 a.m. every morning to go to Mass.

In winter the bitter wind howled around us and the white vapour of our breath hovered about our heads. In the early dawn light, the shuffling queue of girls heading to the chapel looked like ghosts. My knees turned red from kneeling in the cold chapel. I remember noticing Sister Philomena's head bent reverently and I often wondered how she could be so harsh with us all and yet so reverent in church.

But before church, as soon as we were up, we had to make our beds and get dressed. I found that each item in the array of clothes given to us was designed for a specific purpose. One dress was for visitors' days (once a month), one was for play, and the last, a dress in a black and white check pattern, was an everyday school uniform. This small selection of clothes hadn't bothered me at all; I'd never had a big variety. But when it came to under-wear, a girl's personal items were just that—personal.

But now, every second day we changed our day clothes and on alternate days, first thing in the morning, we were lined up to have our underwear inspected. This must have been a fun job for the duty nun, as an obviously pre-calibrated nose was placed close enough to our undies to assess the damage of the previous day. I was never terribly fussy as a child, forever dirty or untidy, but this took personal hygiene to a new level that caused my mouth to open in amazement.

If our undies were clean, we got to turn them inside out and wear them another day. If they were soiled in any way, we visited Sister Philomena.

Sister Philomena's hand would grow magically out of one sleeve and reach into the pocket of her skirt to produce a pink hairbrush. I was to find out what everyone else knew already, that this brush even had a name—Mr Pinky!

Anyone who has ever lived at Nazareth House has felt the back of Mr Pinky on the palms of their hands at some time or other.

Sister Philomena and Mr Pinky were inseparable. Her favourite room for punishment was the bathroom, and from wherever a misdeed was done, an earlobe with a girl attached would be taken to the bathroom to receive due punishment. Most teachers preferred the cane, but for all of us, discipline sat buried in the left-hand pocket of Sister Philomena's habit while her rosary beads stayed in the other one. I sometimes think a more appropriate statue at the front door would have been The Virgin Mary with Beads and Hairbrush.

With the inspection completed, the older girls would dress themselves, and then walk quickly down the endless corridor to dress the smaller ones in the nursery. Sister Rose was in charge of the smaller children. The older children, including myself after a stay of one year and at not quite eight years old, were each assigned to help look after one or two children depending on how many small ones were at the home at the time.

As Sister Rose changed nappies and fussed and cooed to the babies in the nursery, she would call out instructions to us. She was plump, round-faced and very easygoing. Her tight plait, as thick and hard as rope, hung down to her waist and lay hidden inside her habit. She would occasionally smile and let us all feel her plait before shooing us away. We'd hurriedly make the beds assigned to us and then stand in the queue in the corridor for the daily Mass, in those days read in Latin.

Mass completed, we would go to the dining room for breakfast, where the older girls fed the smaller ones their porridge before heading off to school for two hours of religious instruction followed by morning tea.

Our warm milk and jam sandwiches, dry now from being left in the sun, were served in the playground before we were herded back to the classroom for lessons till lunchtime. School resumed at 1 p.m. after lunch, but finished at 2 p.m. when we were walked to the chapel once more for Stations of the Cross and rosaries. After changing out of our school uniforms into play clothes, afternoon tea was served, again in the playground. We were then left to our own devices until dinnertime.

Mealtimes rapidly became unexciting to me after that first much-needed meal. I realise now that most institutions have a strict budget and that basic fare is the easiest and cheapest to prepare. Nazareth House's catering was no exception. Providing food for up to a hundred growing children could not have been easy, and variety was not a vital part of the routine. Still, an active imagination was obviously in play, with mince—the favoured meat—disguised in stews, rissoles and other assorted meals, indicating some deviousness of mind. Other dishes included haddock (a bitter orange fish), sausages or saveloys and, on Fridays, fish fingers. The culinary specialty that led to the most colourful responses and trips to the bathroom was tripe. Desserts, always a highlight of dinner for children, were sago, tapioca, rice pudding or jelly served with custard. They were filling and sweet, and my dream.

After our baths, all clothes were returned to our lockers, prayers were said on our knees by our beds, and the lights were turned out. My favourite nun was Sister Magdalene and she always did our bed check. She was tall and slim, and floated instead of walking. Her face seemed to shine as she smiled and I imagined that this was what an angel looked like: beautiful and serene. In all the years that I spent at the home, she was the only one who ever remembered my birthday with gifts of talcum powder, boxed soap or a prayer card. Anything was special to me. My own hairbrush. My own talcum powder. My own prayer cards.

And that was how our days were filled between Monday and Friday.

Because there were only a few nuns assigned to the children, this routine was possibly the best, and only, way the nuns could keep so many of us in line.

I'm sure that was what my nemesis, Sister Philomena,

thought. She was a very strong disciplinarian, ruling with an iron hand and a wooden brush. She had our days organised, planned as precisely as a military exercise, leaving no time for idleness. Her motto was 'Idle hands are the devil's tools' and if we weren't cleaning or praying, we were sitting quietly knitting beanies and scarves for the cold winter months ahead.

She knew everyone's name and whereabouts at any time of the day—nothing escaped her. I was terrified of her and froze whenever she entered the room or called out my name. On any given weekend, she could be found marching like a general down the corridor with children following behind her resembling a straggly army, on some work detail or other.

One such detail, organised regularly during the summer months, was the weeding of the nuns' cemetery. A group of girls would be taken to pull the weeds and rake up the leaves.

Weeds flourished in the dry ground around the gravesites, and on one occasion, finding these weeds to be very uncooperative, we were told that it was because 'the devil was hanging on to them'. I was always an inquisitive child, asking questions when I should have just accepted what I was told like everyone else, but this statement surprised me.

'Why is the devil down there with the nuns? Haven't they been good enough to go to heaven? Why is the devil hanging on to the weeds?' I asked, my questions coming in rapid succession.

Many times in the future, as on this occasion, when I asked a difficult question, the answer was always 'Sit down and be quiet, Patricia!' During religious instruction, when the story was told of how Adam and Eve had been made by God, of how they'd had children and then those children had children, my question had been, 'Who did they marry?'

I was simply told, 'Sit down, Patricia.'

The same answer was given when I questioned the story of Noah and the Ark. 'Did they marry their sisters and brothers, since everyone else was dead?' I asked innocently.

'Be quiet, Patricia. Why must you always rock the boat?' The look from Sister Philomena had been most disapproving as she dismissed my question with her hand. (I could imagine her saying, 'Don't rock the boat' as she walked through the corridors of the Colosseum leading the Christians to the arena full of lions.) It got to the stage when all I had to do was put my hand up, to be told to be quiet. This became a problem occasionally when I only wanted to be excused to go to the toilet.

I remember during her religion classes, she always said that out of everyone in the world, God would always love us. I often thought that if this were His version of love, I could do without it, thank you very much. My image of Him was of an old man in a white flowing garment sitting on a cloud high above us with an army of angels singing and playing harps while He looked benevolently down on His minions. He must have been so far away that He couldn't see all the pain and suffering that was going on in this world He'd made.

School was conducted in the front room which I had glimpsed on my first night. Two rows of desks faced the blackboard and led away from it to the back of the room. There was a small walkway between rows.

Our classroom behaviour was recorded on the blackboard for all to see. Any slight infringement of rules and a cross would be placed against that child's initials on the board. Woe betide any child whose initials attracted three crosses—that would definitely ensure a visit to Mr Pinky.

The nuns' strategy for ensuring our good behaviour can be summarised by one word: bribery. In the orphanage, where luxuries were almost unheard of, children would turn themselves inside out to earn 'holy cards', which were pictures and stories of popular saints. After receiving one, we would swap favourites the same way children do now with basketball or baseball cards. Holy cards were one of the few items we were allowed to keep as personal possessions. For Sister Philomena, discipline was as simple as black or white—holy cards or Mr Pinky.

I saw the back of Mr Pinky on several occasions during school, more often than not for talking, but occasionally for more creative misdemeanours.

A child's mind is bound to wander if their interest isn't caught and held, and Bible reading was not always the most exciting subject to a seven year old. One morning I remember sitting hunched over, enthralled by colouring all of my fingernails with my lead pencil, until it dawned on me that I could hear the scratching noise I was making above the silence. Startled, I glanced up to find everyone staring at me while Sister Philomena stood in front of me with her arms crossed and lips pursed. By the look on her face I knew I'd earned a visit from Mr Pinky, and with resignation I walked to the bathroom, like Joan of Arc on her way to be burnt at the stake. My punishment that day had been five cuts, 'For your sin of vanity, Patricia,' she said.

We all soon learnt to distinguish the sound of Sister Philomena coming down the corridor towards us. Heard above the warning 'shush' was the clicking of the black beads that served as a belt around her waist and dangled in front of her habit, so that by the time she appeared in the doorway, we had all turned into angels, sitting quietly with our hands folded in front of us.

Religion took up the vast majority of the morning, but afternoons were spent on more conventional studies. I can remember learning to write in copybooks and having the occasional spelling competition. Daily, we all sat hunched over our desks trying to copy the lovely writing shown in our books. To us it looked beautiful and perfect—like a priest had written it. The spelling competitions usually ended in a hotly contested battle between Monica, who had become a close friend, and me.

I remember winning most of these competitions and I was rewarded at the end of the year on Speech Night with a prize for being top of the class. As much as I longed and prayed for a doll of any description, practical prizes in the form of sewing boxes, pencil cases or books were all we ever received. Such prizes were liberally given to all the girls, with categories ranging from best shoelace tier and cleanest girl, to a variety of academic achievements. No-one ever missed out.

These personal prizes given for individual achievement were promptly reclaimed by the nuns at the end of Speech Night and placed in a toy locker. This locker, inaccessible during the week, was opened on Sundays when toys could be played with but had to be returned to the locker again at the end of the day. Any other toys that were brought back from outings or holidays were duly placed in the locker as well, to be shared with everyone.

The joy of Fridays when school ended was marred by the distribution of the regular dose of cod liver oil. (A follow-up of castor oil on Saturday night was given 'to clean us out'.) Still, we all looked forward to the weekends—except for Saturday mornings, which were reserved for floor polishing, a very time-consuming chore assigned to the older children. There were three dormitories and every weekend two details of girls would be given rags, one to wax the floors and one to polish. After breakfast, one group started at the first dormitory where we would drag all the beds (on castor wheels) down to one end, then place a rag with wax on it under our right foot and proceed to wax the floorboards from side to side until we had reached the other end. The second group had clean rags under their feet to shine the floors. We all stood in a row lengthways, arms around each other's waists, as we glided on one foot to the other side and back again, singing the latest popular song of the time. We would then go to the next room and repeat the process, thus filling our first morning off after the school week.

The afternoons were reserved for hair washing and everyone would line up on the grass near the laundry, where huge tubs of water had been placed. After a check for head lice, we would take turns having our heads dunked in the water and washed. Then we were let loose to run like a pack of animals in the paddocks and grounds or allowed to play on the nearby swings until our hair dried. Sometimes, a nun would take us on a supervised walk up to the front gate. We would go in pairs, hand in hand, up and back through the paddock, trying to avoid the many soft cowpats that dotted the grassy slopes.

The last day of the week was reserved for church, rosary saying and confession. Confessions for us were not purely based on our actual misdeeds for the week. Instead, we found ways of enlivening these supposedly deeply religious moments that were not much more than a time-filling exercise for most of us.

We had several visiting priests from Iona or Villanova Colleges (two of the local Catholic boys' schools) but our usual confessor was Father Rudolph, a stooped, grey-haired man of about eighty. He was almost deaf, causing a certain amount of amusement when he took confession. The private conversation whispered from behind closed confessional doors ended up being shouted and echoed throughout the chapel, with all present hearing everything being said—including the details of any sins confessed.

It was on one of these occasions that Mary Williamson went into the confessional to be heard. Mary was one of the older girls who was seemingly always in some sort of trouble.

'Bless me, Father, for I have sinned. It's been one week since my last confession,' could be heard quite clearly by everyone present.

'What are your sins, my child?' bellowed Father Rudolph.

'I've been smoking cigarettes and stealing cars!' was the

fictional confession that reverberated loudly around the chapel, bringing smiles and titters from all the children.

Mary had also been the one who'd taken soap powder from the laundry and put it in the holy water fountain, guaranteeing a lot of her time being spent with Sister Bernard Mary and the strap.

I had very little to do with Sister Bernard Mary, a small nun with a distinctly pear-like body shape. She always seemed to have a frown on her face as she bounced down the corridor on some mission or other. She was in charge of the older girls and was only at the convent for my first year before being transferred to another institution. She was very moody and bad-tempered, as well as prone to using the strap—and her hand, according to some of the girls who had been at the home longer than I had.

Every first Sunday of the month, we put on our best dresses and waited for our families to arrive—hopefully. Each child waited quietly in the playground, either drawing or playing with the toys from the locker, hoping for a nun to come outside and call a name, announcing a visitor. We all held our breaths, anticipating our own name, pleased for the one who had been called but sad to be left behind. I started to hate those Sundays. They were interminable. As I sat among the handful of children not collected, I came to realise that Nazareth House was just a place where parents dumped you and then forgot about you.

In the years that passed, there were only a few visits from my father but never any visits from my mother, and I would wonder many times why not. One visit from my mother was all I wanted. I somehow knew that I would never be going home with Dad because of his bad health, but Mum had been a different story. The only time I'd seen her unwell was when she'd come home drunk at night and woken up sick the next morning. I remember as she lay in bed with a washer over her forehead, making cups of tea and walking as slowly as I could with them, slopping tea over the top of the cup. By the time I reached her, the cup was always half full and a trail of tea led from the kitchen to her bed.

Every month, I waited for her to come and see me. I had a feeling that she was ashamed of me but I still wanted to say I was sorry for always being dirty and breaking things; these childish frailties seemed to annoy her more so than they had Dad. I wanted to say that I would try harder, and then everything would be all right and she'd love me again and take me home. Your mother should love you, shouldn't she?

But she never gave me the opportunity. She never came and I soon stopped asking for her.

I longed for my father so intensely it hurt. He was the most wonderful person in my world. He came as often as he could, not regularly, but I remember those times so well.

I never discussed with him why I was at Nazareth because, firstly, I already knew the answer. Dad was sick and Mum had gone again. Secondly, I would never interrogate my father. If I'd learnt nothing else from the nuns, I'd learnt not to 'rock the boat'. Keep quiet. Be the perfect child. Be lovable. Don't create waves. Don't ask questions. According to the nuns' rule book, if you said a word out of line you were punished, therefore I remained silent. We were all effectively brainwashed into submission and I was too damn scared to say anything in case my father's infrequent visits ceased completely. I never asked him why I was there and he never told me.

So, rightly or wrongly, I accepted my fate. Instead of asking myself 'why?', I asked 'how long?' reasoning that I had been taken back home once before and I would be again. It was just taking longer this time.

I can't remember how much time elapsed before I first saw my father after I'd been deposited at Nazareth House. Almost a year, I think.

The first time my name was called, I thought I had heard incorrectly. I just sat there until my name was called again. Stunned, I was led to the office where I was told to wait for my father. I'd hoped for that moment for so long and now that it had arrived, I couldn't believe it. I felt like I was waiting for a stranger to come for me. Dad existed only in my memory. But when the door of the office opened, I felt myself back in our squalid little flat. What surprised me on that first visit was how much he had aged since I'd last seen him. Still, my heart swelled and I ran to him.

Over the next few years, we would go for walks to the beach, a long way for him and me, but done without any complaint from either of us. Or we would merely sit in the play area with the children who had no visitors, happily drawing and talking for hours before he left to go home. I came to learn that all the nice things are everyday things. Like the smell of his cigarette smoke. The smell wafted over me when he hugged me—it smelt as lovely as perfume.

His budget didn't provide for many special treats, but a train ride to the George Cinema in the city to see *King of Kings*, starring Jeffrey Hunter as Jesus, was one I'll never forget. We had lunch afterwards and then headed back to the home by train again. I had a tremendous crush on Jeffrey Hunter for years after seeing that movie.

And then there was that memorable day when Queensland's largest yearly country fair, the Exhibition, came to Brisbane. A fair or carnival is always a treat for children, so Dad had planned a surprise trip for me.

The main arena with its displays of farm animals, the horse-and-buggy races and fireworks, combined with the noise and fun of stomach-churning rides at sideshow alley, appealed to everyone from two to eighty-two. Sample bags and every type of junk food a kid could want were all readily available. At eleven years old, I thought this place was heaven.

That Saturday, Dad and I walked around all day eating hot-dogs and drinking strawberry milkshakes with another two adults, a man and a woman who I suppose would have been in their early twenties. I had no idea who these people were but they seemed to be friends of Dad's. They walked around with us, while the lady smiled at me and held my hand through sideshow alley.

Dad left me with them that night but returned the next day to take me back to the home. I don't remember doing much in particular during my stay besides walking around their small garden and hanging over the fence looking at passing cars on the busy street. Sunday looked to be a sleep-in day for them so I kept to myself, which I really didn't mind at all. Survival for me meant being unobtrusive and keeping a low profile anyway. I was away from the home and that was a treat in itself.

Days later, back at the home, we were told that those who'd gone out for the weekend could write a letter of thanks and it would be posted for us, so I bent my head to the task. I poured my thanks out effusively, trying to ingratiate myself with the couple I'd visited in the hope of future weekends with them or possibly permanent placement.

When I think of that letter I marvel at my naivety. I couldn't remember the couple's names or where they lived but that didn't faze me. I simply addressed the letter to 'The man and the lady who live in the white house on the corner of the busy street at Milton'. Sort of like writing to Santa Claus.

But amazingly, it seemed to work. Three days later in the playground, mail call was on and my name was called out. In all the years I'd been at Nazareth House, that had never happened before. No-one had ever sent me a letter or even so much as a birthday card. Never.

Sister Philomena stood holding a small bundle of letters in her hand. As I walked up to her with a huge smile on my face, I looked around at the other children to see if everyone was watching me collect mail from someone who cared enough to send me a letter. I saw envious faces, expectant faces and some unhappy ones who knew there would be nothing for them. Some children looked bored, simply shuffling their feet, wanting to go back to what they'd been doing.

Sister handed my mail to me in an offhand manner and continued calling names. I clutched it preciously to my chest and walked back to my place, anticipating the moment when I could sit down and read it alone but I couldn't stop myself from glancing down at the envelope then and there.

My happiness evaporated when I saw the words 'Return to Sender' stamped across the front of the envelope. Not wanting to believe what I'd read, I tore open the letter and, sure enough, saw my own writing on the pages that I unfolded.

Cautiously, I looked up to see if anyone was watching me, while keeping a smile firmly planted on my face. I didn't tell anyone. I wanted them all to think that I was loved and wanted. Even though the pain was immense, the humiliation if my secret were ever found out would have been worse.

I remember glancing up at Sister Philomena as I fought to hold back the tears, thinking that she would have been better off looking after lepers than raising children. She never even looked at me, never displayed a flicker of emotion—nothing that would have softened the blow for me. Hadn't she seen the front of the envelope? Surely she'd seen 'Return to Sender' stamped boldly on the front. Would it have been so hard to have pulled me aside later and explain to me why it had been returned?

I never found out whether she was really as cold-hearted as she seemed or whether it was just a veneer of aloofness. These days I can afford the luxury of giving her a little latitude. What seemed like coldness could actually have been necessary emotional self-preservation. I've often wondered if any of the nuns initially got too involved with the plight of the children but eventually learnt to distance themselves from their emotions, a strategy that a child would see as uncaring. I've often tried to put myself in their situation and I think it would have driven me crazy. Like working in an animal refuge and watching pain and suffering day after day.

What the nuns didn't realise was that all we wanted from them was love. Nothing more, nothing less.

One of the few relatives I visited was Dad's cousin, who I called 'Aunty Mary'. She lived in one of the outer suburbs of Brisbane in a house that looked as if the next gust of wind would blow it over. What fascinated me the most was her outside toilet, situated in a small building in the backyard and called an 'outhouse'. It didn't have a chain to flush like the one at Nazareth House. Instead, on the floor was a box full of sawdust to scoop into the toilet, which got emptied only once a week.

The one time I saw her, Aunty Mary clasped her hands together and smiled at me as she said, 'Look how much you've grown. When I last saw you, you were two years old. You looked like a little doll barely tall enough to walk, but instead you ran everywhere.'

When Dad took me back to the home, I was always quiet. He would look at me and say, 'Do you feel all right?'

How could I tell him how I felt? Unloved? Unwanted? Rejected?

When I went back to the home, all joy left me and I wanted to run back to him and be loved again. I wanted to feel his arms around me as I lay against his chest forever.

I wanted to say to him, 'Don't leave me.'

But he always did.

These occasional personal outings with Dad supplemented the rare group outings at Nazareth House, which were available only for the ones deemed to be 'well behaved'.

Once every couple of months, we would all line up like little soldiers and walk what seemed like miles, but was actually only about 400 metres, to the local train station for a ride to Wynnum Central, the hub of Moreton Bay. It was then only a short walk from the train station to the main road, Edith Street.

This metropolis had two blocks of small shops and offices facing each other across the road, separated by little service alleys which ran around the back of the buildings. There was a barbershop, a doctor's office, a couple of jewellery stores, some coffee shops, one ladies' and one men's outfitters and the main grocery store, Woolworths.

On the street, there was no protection from the blazing sun or the rain. There were benches on the footpaths, but they were always empty.

And that was it. There was never anything much going on.

We had been given one shilling (today's equivalent of ten cents) back at the home and on arrival at Wynnum we were set loose in Woolworths with strict instructions on conduct, behaviour and meeting time. When our money had been spent on bags of lollies, we returned. We became very astute buyers, only spending our pittance on boiled sweets that could be sucked indefinitely, thus lasting longer than the much-coveted chocolate. We also learnt to ration ourselves when eating our sweets, because no-one knew if they could stay well behaved enough to be included in the next excursion.

The untimely demise of a prominent local Catholic religious figure, Archbishop Duhig of Brisbane, had provided us with an unscheduled trip to St Stephens Cathedral in the city. The fact that this visit involved viewing an open casket, for those who were inclined to pay their last respects, resulted in a slightly reduced level of excitement.

It was on this occasion that my friend Monica and I, and another girl, Christine, were told that we had been chosen as the best behaved and would accompany Sister Philomena and two other nuns in the convent station wagon to view the mortal remains of Archbishop Duhig. Over the years, I had stopped bashing my head against the wall in rebellion and starting conforming to the day-to-day rules of the nuns. I could now be classed as well behaved.

So there we were, lined up in our Sunday best (our school uniforms were pronounced not good enough). Our underwear had been sniffed and our good shoes inspected. A large hole had been found in the sole of one of my shoes, so a piece of paper was quickly coloured black and placed inside my shoe to ensure that when I knelt in the pew, the person behind me would not have an offensive insight into my 'sole'. It was obviously important that I was 'un-holey' on this holy occasion.

On arrival at St Stephens we made our way forward slowly in the queue, finally arriving at the casket to look at someone who, on the evidence available, clearly had not yet gone to heaven. After all, hadn't we been promised that when you die, if you have been good, you go to heaven? Archbishop Duhig obviously had not been as good as he should have been because there he was, looking sound asleep and certainly not in heaven yet.

Just then, a nun next to me leant over and whispered, 'Kiss him, Patricia.'

I was horrified.

'But he's dead,' I stated rather unnecessarily.

'The ring,' she said in an exasperated voice. 'Kiss the ring.'

I looked down again. I noticed that his arms were over his chest in the shape of a cross, just like mine every night, and I wondered if the black dogs followed you into heaven if you didn't cross your arms.

With a jab in the back from the next nun, I duly kissed his hand and sat down, waiting for the rest of the entourage to pay their respects while I looked around and remembered my times here at school when I lived with my parents. To the left of the entrance was the baptismal font where I had been baptised in Grade 1. And I remembered in Grade 2 walking up the aisle wearing my white communion dress and lace veil, lent to me by the nuns on my first communion day. I remembered smiling at my parents as I walked past them up to the altar.

It all seemed so long ago. My world had changed since then. I had gone on to another life.

All too soon, we were on our way back. At the home, we were the centre of attention. The three of us basked in it until after lunch, when we discovered to our amazement that every-one else would now be going to the cathedral in the school bus while we had earned the dubious privilege of being left behind to clean up everyone's dirty lunch dishes.

As I washed and Christine and Monica dried, I turned to them and said quite seriously, 'I'm never being good again.'

Aside from these rare outings, yearly concerts were performed close to Christmas for relatives of the children and provided us with another break in routine. I cannot remember any Christmas decorations or trees during those years. Through the buzz of excitement our chores continued as usual until our holiday foster parents eventually picked us up.

We would practise our Irish jigs and sword dances daily, with our hands clenched and arms glued to our sides while being encouraged to 'lift those knees' by Sister Philomena. Performing surprisingly nimble steps for someone of her size, she would stand with right heel tucked into her left instep forming a 'T', and proceed to hop from toe to toe with veil flying and a rosy glow in her cheeks while keeping perfect time to the music. These were practically the only times I saw her smiling.

As well as this dancing, a select dozen girls between the ages of five and sixteen were chosen for the choir. Marilyn, a girl who arrived when I had already been there a year and who left a year before my own departure, was the eldest in this group, and as such was chosen to lead the choir.

On arrival at Nazareth House, we had each been given the regulation near-military haircut, but Marilyn's, for some reason, was even more severe. Her hair had been long and wavy, but the nuns had shorn it so close to her head that she had to wear a babushka until some semblance of recovery growth had started. It was fairly obvious that none of the nuns were hairdressers before joining the convent; all of us sported short, uneven hair and looked much like convicts.

Marilyn, in charge of the choir, took her role seriously and promptly took on the task of giving singing lessons to the youngest ones, something we all could have used—even her. But it was in these early years that my love of music surfaced and I became aware of the happiness it could bring. Even today, Irish ballads bring tears to my eyes and a lump to my throat.

Just prior to our Christmas extravaganza, the event everyone looked forward to was a picnic on the beach, organised and paid for by the local parishioners. Boxes full of swimming costumes, all of them old and tatty, were dug up from the bowels of the convent and distributed amongst the children with little consideration being given to colour or size. We usually spent the first hour after receiving our costumes trying to adjust them by tying the straps in a knot on top of each shoulder or tying the backs together with anything we could find, in an attempt at modesty.

We would all be taken to the beach at Wynnum, such as it

was, where Santa arrived on the back of a trailer distributing bags of lollies to everyone. We were given soft drinks and cake, unheard of at Nazareth, and played for hours in the concrete-enclosed saltwater pool on the beach or on the swings nearby. None of us knew how to swim so we simply splashed around in the water. We were also allowed to walk to the end of the jetty where we could see the fishermen coming in with their catch. Ugly wet fish still hung on the end of lines.

At the end of the day, we came back exhausted, sunburnt and happy after this break in routine. Such wonderful events were enjoyed by all of us but were very few and far between. All too quickly we were back to the reality of life in an orphanage with all its associated order and discipline.

Each nun had her own way of keeping the children under control.

Sister Bernard Mary was very physical, choosing to discipline with a strap or the back of her hand, as Mary Williamson had found out (via a burst eardrum and subsequent partial deafness in one ear.)

Sister Philomena's technique was more psychological. She preferred to prevent wrongdoing with demonic tales that instilled terror in young, impressionable girls and guaranteed good behaviour no matter what the situation. This was her way of teaching us not to be greedy, vain or jealous of each other and that as long as we repented our sins, God would forgive us.

For all the nuns' teachings of an all-loving, all-forgiving God, what I craved more than anything in those years were physical affection and love, both in short supply at Nazareth. Outward signs of affection such as touching and holding hands were frowned upon; even sisters were separated and encouraged to mix with other children rather than spend time with each other.

This caused real heartaches for children already trying to attune themselves to a new way of life. A set of five-year-old twins, Marianne and Antoinette, never fully adjusted and could always be found sitting together holding hands in out-of-the-way corners, hoping the nuns wouldn't find them.

From my experience with Catholic institutions, they seemed to be short on warmth and long on Jesus. While I tried to make the most of my situation (I had no other choice), some children never adjusted to this institutional life.

CHAPTER 5

---✛---

The Chameleon

'I forgot to tell you that Dad rang while you were shopping,' said Tony. He was always either forgetting to pass on messages or getting messages wrong.

I was on fairly good terms with my ex-husband, but it was now 8 p.m., my feet were screaming from standing on them all day, and I was looking forward to a cup of coffee and just spending some quality time with the boys.

'Do you know what he wanted?' I didn't really want to call him back but if it was important, I knew I would probably have to.

'He didn't say much but he did mention he had a phone call from someone called Sandra Stewart.'

The name meant nothing to me. 'And?' I said.

'He said that she thinks she's your sister.'

I stood dumbfounded for what felt like five minutes but was probably only five seconds. I didn't quite know what to say. I managed to stammer, 'Are you sure he said those exact words?'

'I think so. But he wants you to ring him back tonight.'

Tony could not know just what those words meant to me. *'She thinks she's your sister.'*

I mumbled something to the boys about having to go to the bathroom and after wandering in a daze down the hallway found myself sitting on my bed.

I remembered the first time a sister was mentioned. It had made no sense to me. But then again, my whole life had seemed to make no sense. It had been a period when I had almost given up. Trying to get rid of these memories from my mind was like trying to scoop mercury up with a fork. They held years of rejection, pain, hurt and anger, and would never fully leave me. That's what's so unfair. So very unfair. Thirty years of mentally denying these events made everything a little hazy, yet now those few words made it all come back in horrid vividness and clarity.

Although the lack of visible and physical love was only too evident to me during my time at Nazareth House, if asked now the one thing I would have changed, it would not be that.

At the time of a child's life when they're fast becoming aware of themselves and others, the selection of suitable foster parents is crucial. In the 1950s and 1960s, the process did not have the more stringent controls that are in place these days. Today, there are interviews with prospective parents, visits from social workers, checks done on financial status, not to mention an interminable waiting list before all of this even starts. In those days, being Catholic was assumed to carry with it all the requirements for being a suitable foster family.

Believe me, this was not always the case.

Practising Catholics, who are taught from an early age 'to give rather than to receive' and that 'the heart is happiest when it beats for others', were asked or volunteered to take orphaned and abandoned children into their homes during school holidays for periods of up to six weeks. By and large, these teachings are wonderful tenets to hold in life, and have often inspired other Christians to help those who were not as well off as themselves. And for the most part, these people believed they were doing an unselfish Christian deed by breaking the day-to-day monotony for the children and giving them something to look forward to. Sadly, some foster parents were unprepared for the psychological problems that many of the children carried inside them as a result of the situations they came from.

There were children who had come from shattered families where one parent had died, leaving the other parent unable to cope with one or more children on their own. Putting them in the home was the only way of handling this situation, with the understanding that it was merely temporary. Marilyn had been one of those girls.

Others, like me, were in for the long haul.

I knew by now that I would never be going back home. With a father who was constantly sick and a mother who had virtually disappeared, my chances of returning to them were negligible. My only hope for leaving the orphanage was to be fostered. I knew that without being told.

Although many of us harboured feelings of abandonment and rejection and most of us lacked self-confidence, what was common among all of us was a craving for acceptance. These holiday visits turned me into a little actress, thinking I was on display for people who were choosing a child to stay with them permanently. I knew that, as I grew older, it was more and more unlikely that someone would want me since most people wanted small children who could be passed off as their own. I had seen this happen on numerous occasions and at eight years old, I knew my chances of being chosen were becoming less and less. I had no idea of where my future lay. The future for me was tomorrow or the next day.

I went to a series of holiday foster homes until I was nearly twelve, each time put into a 'do or die' situation where desperation overshadowed the happiness that these people had intended for me in the first place. I went with high hopes, wishing desperately that they would see something in me that they liked and therefore decide to keep me.

Once inquisitive and happy, my growing uncertainty about my future made me a quiet and insecure child who would initially sit and watch, listening for any indication whatsoever of the kind of child they preferred. I learnt to watch hard and long, observing, noting and calculating while trying to interpret every possible nuance from the way they talked or even folded their arms. With this in mind, I changed more often than a chameleon.

If they wanted a bubbly, outgoing child—I would be exactly that. If they wanted a studious child who read quietly and stayed out of the way—fine by me! If they wanted a cute little girl who played with dolls and had tea parties—no worries!

I changed my personality constantly and tried to mould myself into their perfect child. I carried with me more personalities than a politician, ready to ingratiate myself into their lives. I was undemanding, tidy, always clean, and a happy, laughing child, doing all my chores without complaint. Nothing was too much for me.

I was the child anyone would want.

One small but terribly important piece of information not passed on to the children by the nuns was that these people only wanted to have a child for the holiday period. Not knowing this, it seemed no matter how hard I tried, I just wasn't good enough. I was always returned. At the end of every stay, we would pull up at the main entrance of the home and I would be out of their car and walking stoically up the stairs to the doorbell with my head held high before they had even closed their car doors.

I tried to show them all I didn't care, but I can't pretend it didn't hurt deep down because it certainly did; it was yet another rejection and I hurt like hell. Every time, I died a little inside, again and again. Nobody ever wanted me. I was starting to feel like I was going through a revolving door; no sooner out than back again.

I was first introduced to some of the seedier characters of this

world at the age of seven. The Conlons were once my parents'
landlords, and as such were one set of the early foster parents
selected for a visit, since I was already familiar with them. Mr
Conlon was married with a son a little younger than I was and for
a little while, the attention he gave me was very welcome. He
would offer to wash and dress me until, even at that young age, I
started feeling uncomfortable with the detail and extent of the
washing routine.

One night, as dinner was being prepared by his wife and Mr
Conlon read to his son and me on the double bed, he tried
working his hand down inside my pants.

I had no idea what was on his mind. My only thoughts
were, *This is a bad touch.* I wanted it to stop; instinctively knowing this shouldn't be happening. I crossed my legs tightly to
prevent further exploration.

Through all of my young life, the only people I had ever
been afraid of were the nuns who had my respectful fear, but
never 'normal' people, until Mr Conlon put his hand up my skirt
and hurt me with his fingers.

I ran into the kitchen clinging to Mrs Conlon. My visit with
them was suddenly cut short and I was returned to the home
shortly after this incident, never visiting them again, but left with
a feeling that I was the one being punished and consequently
should be ashamed of myself.

It seemed as if a pattern was starting to form when at
another home bathing the children was again done by the foster
father. He would wash me last, insisting that 'all my crevices' were
properly cleaned, eventually sending me into fits of tears every
afternoon when bathtime was announced.

Another time, I remember waking up in the middle of the
night to find a 'giving Catholic foster father' standing at my bed-
side naked; his only comment being 'Just touch me'. I turned my
back to him and prayed desperately that he would go away as I
lay curled up in a foetal position for what seemed like half an

hour, too scared to move, listening to his breathing. Eventually I heard his footsteps retreating back to his bed.

I barely slept for the rest of that night. I lay awake until I saw the slight change in the shadows that meant dawn was approaching.

Over the years, after similar instances with other foster fathers, a change in me gradually started to set in. I'd tried to be good, but I somehow knew that good behaviour wasn't all they wanted and I would be soon sent back. I became angry and bitter, a picture of defiance and filled with a dark rage, something that didn't go unnoticed by the nuns.

Sister Philomena's solution to this, and almost every problem, was more work. It was decided that I was now old enough to help change the bed linen in the aged section of the home every afternoon when school had finished and again every Saturday morning, on top of my other chores, which included bathing the younger children at night.

I'd become a tough, cynical eleven year old and a handful to control, but by now I'd seen too much to care. I'd learnt to shut down and not react any more—just like a circuit breaker.

This was the sullen, angry child who greeted the Andersons during the Christmas of 1967. Theirs was to be the last foster home I visited. They were to find that inside, I was a far cry from the sweet, innocent child they thought they were getting when they collected me from Nazareth House to take me to their home over the Christmas holidays.

CHAPTER 6

✛

Deadcliffe

The Andersons lived on the Redcliffe Peninsula, about thirty kilometres north of Brisbane and more affectionately known to the youth who lived there as 'Deadcliffe'. It was mainly a retirement area in those days with very few facilities for the growing young population, just a pebbly beach sheltered from the surf by nearby islands. Its only saving grace was that it was cooler than Brisbane in the summer and a little warmer in winter because of the ocean breezes.

After crossing over a bridge called the Hornibrook Highway, we drove quite a long way to a suburb called Scarborough, turning left into Bennett Street and driving a short distance before pulling into a driveway.

Hugging to my chest the small case containing my three changes of clothes, I stepped out of the car and looked around.

The house had a small front yard, closed in on both sides by a six-foot fence. A low white picket fence at the front shielded a row of annual flowers. Small stones had been used as a border between the coarse grass and the flower beds. Overhanging the whole front yard was a poinciana tree, not as big as the one at

Nazareth House, but greener and bushier, obviously better cared for. The house was high-set with stairs that led up from the side to the front door.

As I was led through the compact house to one of the three bedrooms, my impression was that it was all comfortable and clean.

There was a huge grand piano which dominated the lounge room. The other half of the L-shaped room held lounge chairs and a TV. All our meals were eaten at the table in the kitchen.

The Andersons were an older couple in their mid-fifties who had both been married previously. There was only one child from Mrs Anderson's former marriage, a son who was married with children of his own.

Mr Anderson worked for the Brisbane City Council and travelled an hour each way daily to Brisbane and back, arriving home at 6.30 p.m. to a meal on the table by 6.35 p.m. He was a nondescript, portly man at merely five-foot four, with only a little grey hair left on his balding head.

Mrs Anderson was a very patient but firm woman. She needed to be if she was to handle me. She gave me chores to do—helping to prepare meals every night, doing dishes and helping with the ironing and laundry—all of which I had already been doing in the home so it was just a matter of course for me. My days were filled, and at night I was allowed one hour of television if all my chores had been completed, and then it was into bed by 7.30 p.m. where I could read if I wanted.

As well as me, a Malaysian boy by the name of Adam lived with the Andersons. He was a sweet-natured child, adopted at birth and now five years old, who won me over on my first day by smiling and winking at me whenever he caught my eye. We both regarded the Andersons as grandparents more than parents, not just because of their age, but because Mrs Anderson's grandchildren were all my age or older.

In the next few weeks, I learnt a little about Mr Anderson.

He fussed over small things. The towels on the bathroom rack had to be perfectly straight. The kitchen sink had to be dried completely—all suds and water were to be mopped up to leave a gleaming sink. When I dusted, all items were to be placed exactly where I had found them—dead centre. He was so proud of his handwriting. It was neat and precise, and he laboured to make every stroke perfect. Now, I would call it pedantic, which matched his personality completely.

Many times, he sat with me on the stool in front of the piano keyboard to teach me how to play. He said I had the perfect hands for playing the piano—long fingers that could easily span a full octave even at my young age. As much as I would have loved to learn, the thought of sitting on the stool close to him (or anyone) every day for an hour or more was something I couldn't bring myself to do. I cringed at the touch of another person. I wouldn't even let them kiss or hug me goodnight.

Maybe I presented a challenge to the Andersons because by the end of that Christmas break, they decided that they would keep me—surprisingly, because with them, I had decided not to try at all. I remember asking myself, *What's the use, I'll be going back to Nazareth House anyway.*

Out of the blue, I faced a problem I hadn't anticipated. *What will Dad think when he goes to the home and I'm not there? How will he know where I am and that I don't want to be here?*

It seemed that there was nothing I could do about it.

The Andersons had been unaware of what had happened to me over the past few years, only observing that I was withdrawn, distrustful and suspicious of everyone, and that I saw ulterior motives in everything done for me. I had built a barrier around myself, believing that if I kept everyone outside it I wouldn't be hurt any more.

I became aware that they had previously fostered three other girls before me; all had left at early ages and were not heard of again. The exception was Jennifer, who had married young and lived thirty minutes away. Although she'd never had any children of her own, she had a toy poodle that she regularly dyed apricot and treated like a baby, dressing it in pretty coats and putting bows in its hair.

Because of my small selection of clothes, Jennifer took pity on me, and gave me dresses and shorts that she no longer wanted. I remember thanking her and being so happy to have so many lovely things to wear. The fact that they were all too big was totally lost on me. Most of the dresses hung down to below my knees, accentuating my pigeon toes and bandy, skinny legs. But they were so pretty and the colours were bright.

Mrs Anderson adored Jennifer, and we went to see her quite regularly. Shortly after I started living with the Andersons, Jennifer gave me some insight into my near future. Looking at me seriously with her hand on my shoulder, she said, 'Listen to me. I want you to come to me straight away if anything ever happens that you don't like. Anything at all.'

I wish I had understood then what I was to understand all too well later.

My seventh school year at the only local Catholic girls' school in Redcliffe, Saint Bernadette's, turned out to be very difficult for me, resulting in a basic pass as I struggled with a curriculum that was vastly different from that of Nazareth House.

I could recite freely from the Bible, knowing parts of it almost backwards, and I knew all about the lives of many of the canonised saints, but I could barely add two numbers together and arrive at the correct answer. It seemed that teaching, as well as hairdressing, was deficient at the home. Many nights before exams were spent sitting with Mrs Anderson while I repeated the 'times table' over and over until both of us were thoroughly exhausted.

Making friends at school had also been a problem for me. I made myself an island: indifferent and uninterested in their mindless banter and showing no sense of humour. At lunchtime, I ate my food. When schoolwork was given, I took advice from the teachers but I was reluctant to stand up and ask if I didn't understand something. I preferred to work and worry it out myself. When it was time to go home, I walked alone, and at night I lay with my eyes open staring at the ceiling. I blended. Became common and unremarkable. Unnoticed.

I much preferred being by myself than with a group of giggling girls, which resulted in some of them interpreting this as snobbishness.

If they only knew. I had very little to be snobbish about.

Mrs Anderson suggested that I call them Mum and Dad now that I was to stay with them permanently. I couldn't. Other foster parents had asked me to call them that and I'd done it just to please them. I had called so many women 'Mum' in my life; I just couldn't bring myself to refer to yet another woman by that name. I didn't want these people to be my parents so I simply waited until they looked at me before I would speak.

I used to look around at the other girls laughing and smiling with their mothers, holding hands and looking so happy. It wasn't as if I didn't have a mum. I did. Then I would look at Mrs Anderson. I didn't want this old lady to be my mother. I wanted my own mother. Why didn't she want me? Was I so unlovable?

As for Mr Anderson, he had no hope of living up to my father.

I imagined my life to be just a nightmare—something I'd wake up from in my own bed at home. It would be the morning that I hadn't smelt tea and toast—the morning I'd gone to school by myself. This time, I wouldn't go. This time I would hide like I had other times and no-one would be able to find me. My life would be different and I wouldn't be here now. It amazed me to think that the course of my life may have been altered by that one simple decision.

But it wasn't a dream. This nightmare was my life.

It was at this time that I discovered the library, becoming an avid reader of any whodunits I could lay my hands on, starting with Agatha Christie. I don't remember ever going to the Children's Section. The mysteries held me spellbound. By accident, I saw a book with the face of a beautiful woman on the cover. *Rebecca*. I deviated from whodunits to read it and was transported into a world of mystery, love, romance and passion. From there, I couldn't stop. *Jane Eyre*. *Little Women*. *Lorna Doone*. The wonderful *Wuthering Heights* and the magnificent Heathcliff. The trivia of Mills and Boon romances did not interest me. I needed something with substance. I'd sit quietly and read for hours, totally absorbed in the story, oblivious to anything that was happening around me. It felt good pretending to be someone else in another time and place. I never felt alone or lonely while I had a book in my hand. I was never happier than when I lost myself completely in the life of the hero or heroine, dreaming of a life that was anything but the misery mine really was.

Surprisingly, I passed my exams in Year 7 and progressed into Year 8, commencing at St Bernadette's 'sister' high school, Soubirous College, yet another Catholic school for girls. This was again a close religious atmosphere, barely different from Nazareth House, with Brigidine nuns for teachers and Mass held three times a week. I soon learnt that, possibly as in most institutions, rules were rules and if you obeyed, you would be fine.

One strict rule that we were made to adhere to was the dress code. Our uniform was a simple dark green tunic over a brown blouse, a green belt, black shoes and stockings. As soon as we stepped outside the school grounds, we were to wear a tie (with school badge attached), hat and gloves at all times, only adding the school blazer during the cold winter months.

Every Monday morning, we were lined up on parade where we knelt on the concrete waiting our turn for a prefect, armed with a ruler, to measure the required two inches from ground to hem. I'm sure the nuns were unaware that this procedure didn't bother us at all, since as soon as we were out of sight of the school we simply bloused our skirts over the top of our belts, bringing the hem up to the scandalously short lengths we all liked.

I was again perceived as a 'loner' and drama class was the choice of the nuns to bring me into a group atmosphere where I could learn to interact with other girls. Although I had no trouble remembering lines and cues and I loved the idea of pretending to be someone else (I'd had enough practice), one major obstacle stopped me from doing well in this class—I was extremely shy and lacking in confidence. I considered myself to be a 'beige' person, blending into the background rather than bringing attention to myself. I wasn't prepared to open myself to what I thought would only be criticism or ridicule, so I found it safer just to sit and watch, hiding my inner turmoil.

It was discovered during this class that I could also hold a tune. I was no prodigy but I had good pitch and I loved music. So deciding that drama may not have been the best choice after all, the nuns had me join the choir, where I could blend into a group and sing as well.

On reflection, this was probably the best thing that could have happened to me, as it was the first step towards making friends at the school. I finally started to feel accepted, giving me the badly needed confidence that I'd lacked, and I began to laugh again. From there, I was asked to join sporting activities such as swimming, tennis and athletics.

Everyone had been allocated to different sporting teams, called 'houses', that were named after religious themes. Bon Secoeur was blue, Lourdes was red and Fatima was yellow. I was a Fatima girl, and even though we were the loudest supporters, we never failed to come anywhere but last.

Everyone competed enthusiastically in all sports but the school favourite (though not mine) was definitely swimming, with training being held daily between 5 a.m.–6 a.m. and 4 p.m.–5 p.m.

We all regarded this harrowing schedule in addition to school studies and homework as a form of torture devised by the nuns, and surely best left to the truly dedicated or talented. I declared quite honestly that I was neither.

Mr Cusak, our swimming coach, would walk up and down the side of the Olympic-size pool, barking out instructions to improve our swimming form or, in my case, lack of form. While he was renowned for his patience and persistence as well as attaining extremely good results from most of the girls, I'm sure he had never seen the likes of me before. He soon found out that I was certainly no Shane Gould.

Freestyle I could cope with, but I never seemed to gain much forward momentum with breaststroke and would be left far behind in the pool as the gap between the others and myself widened. Fortunately, there were no lifeguards at our swimming meets, as I'm sure there would have been an attempt to rescue me during my butterfly display and my directionally uncontrollable backstroke. Lane markers as well as other girls were always in danger of being sideswiped as I invariably skewed all over the pool while performing both of these strokes.

My friend, Therese Pilgrim, and I would swim our hearts out for our house while also having a private competition between the two of us. She persistently won the bet by coming second-last, but no matter how hard I tried I always came second . . . to Therese Pilgrim.

I was finally saved from the starting blocks when Mrs Anderson noticed that my fair hair was getting a decidedly green tinge from the chlorine in the pool and that unfeminine Atlas-like shoulders were forming on my small frame.

Maybe there was a God after all, because I much preferred the newly allocated ball sports to swimming. We were all encouraged to participate in everything no matter what sport we preferred, but tennis was my favourite. A club was organised where weekend games were played at different schools (Catholic girls' schools, of course), but during the week the lunch bell produced a scurry of twenty or more girls all trying to be the first onto one of the two tennis courts near the play area.

None of us had any time to change out of our school uniforms and into our sports clothes before the game. In summer, sweat-soaked armpits and an invisible cloud of body odour made it obvious who had played tennis and who had been smart enough to sit in the shade near the tuckshop.

The agreed rules were that the first two girls on the court for that lunch period, be it little lunch or big lunch, could choose their own partner and had the court for all or part of lunch, at their own discretion. As soon as the bell went, we forgot all the lessons the nuns had taught us about being refined young Catholic ladies as we turned into screaming harridans, pushing and shoving everyone out of our way and waving our tennis racquets high above our heads, yelling, 'Me first! Outta my way! Get lost!'

The irony of this was that the class immediately preceding lunch was 'Deportment and Etiquette'.

I was always competitive, striving to do my best in everything, and schoolwork was no exception. I tried very hard to receive good marks in all my subjects, eventually coming consistently in the top ten of my class after deciding to take an academic course. I was told this course would give me more of a range of future professions. Although Latin (which I hated) was my best subject, I can truthfully say that none of my subjects gave me too much concern, except for Physics, which, contrary to popular belief, seemed to have no logic whatsoever.

By the end of Year 9 and with the equivalent of an 'A' today, I decided to change from Latin to Typing, concluding that the latter had more scope and practical use. This decision caused Sister St Jude to place both hands over her heart and stare at me in utter disbelief while exclaiming, 'Oh no, not TYPING, Patricia!' I had been her pet because I had learnt her beloved

Latin with ease, but from then on, whenever she saw me, she would shake her head and frown disbelievingly at me.

More important than any school subject was a woman's attributes. A figure, manners, deportment, elocution. All of these would guarantee a quality marriage. In those days, that was the best a young woman could hope for. It was a man's world. I grew up with these sorts of values—where women were judged like that. I felt gauche, stumbling, unappealing and unattractive. I had no hope. I was plain and dowdy.

All studies and sports were designed to ensure we had healthy minds and bodies. To balance this with a healthy soul we had Father Frawley, our parish priest, who was usually assisted by a 'trainee priest' (a curate). In the few years I was at Soubirous College, curates seemed to come and go quite rapidly.

On one occasion, a young, good-looking, fair-haired curate, Father Kennedy, more like a movie star than a priest, arrived at Soubirous, and sent the college full of pubescent girls into a head spin. He must have been the hardest working priest in Queensland with each girl going to confession three times a day with sins concocted to shock him. This, I am sure, enlivened his life and generally raised the temperature in the confessional box.

During his sermons, we all sat dreamily looking at him, none of us hearing a word he said. He could have told us Jesus was a Martian and we would have believed him.

If the hierarchy had thought more about it, they would have realised that ours was probably the wrong school for him. After only two weeks, Father Frawley sent him away to avoid continued disruption—none of which was really his fault. His replacement was an elderly priest who wouldn't send our hearts and newly developed hormones racing as he looked at us over his spectacles. He left no doubt that he would not stand for any such behaviour, assuming we even wanted to engage in it.

Along with racing hormones came the onset of my menstrual cycle, all of which brought many confusing emotions as rules and restrictions became extremely stringent at home.

At school, we were given lectures, shown movies, and a nurse even visited our class to explain what would be happening to our bodies. Everyone had been given a sample pack of sanitary napkins to take home so that when this 'happy and blessed event' occurred, we would all be prepared. Even though I was aware of this forthcoming process, its actual arrival came as a shock, and for some reason unknown to me then and now, my feelings were that I was dirty. For me, this event was something to hide, not rejoice in!

I'd had three menstrual cycles before Mrs Anderson discovered blood on my knickers one washday and the truth finally came out. On previous occasions, to buy pads at the corner shop on the way home from school, I'd had to secretly take money out of Mrs Anderson's purse, adding more tension to an already stressful situation because I was now waiting to be found out for that as well. The sword of Damocles was hanging over me again.

She was very hurt and confused about why I had hidden this from her. Even I didn't know why I had, but she diplomatically dropped the subject.

With the onset of my periods came other changes in my body that I didn't like. While my puppy fat dropped off me almost overnight it seemed, and my body started filling out everywhere, all my clothes became loose in some places and tight in others. For the first time I had a waist, rounded hips and breasts, something that bothered rather than pleased me.

I felt conspicuous and was sure people were looking at me. One person certainly was—Mr Anderson.

He tried to find reasons to pass me in the small hallway, and started to reach out his hand to touch me as we passed. As he touched my breast once, he crudely said, 'Your headlights are on.'

At the time, I couldn't believe he was doing something that

I thought was so blatantly obscene. The next time he touched me, the reaction he got was certainly not the one he expected.

I had no idea where this fear came from. It started like a fist in the pit of my stomach, clutched my heart then bubbled out hysterically as I screamed and flailed my arms around my head, yelling, 'Don't touch me, just don't touch me!'

Mrs Anderson had no idea how to console me. She left me to sit on the hallway floor, my back against the wall, knees up to my chin and my forehead resting on them, sobbing uncontrollably as my heart pounded in my chest.

I had been confused and shocked at the intensity of what I was feeling and had no idea of what was happening to me or why; I just wanted to be left alone. I closed my eyes. Somewhere out there, life made sense.

Mr Anderson didn't dare come near me. I made my face hard as I looked at him and it was enough to make him lower his eyes and walk quietly away.

That glimpse of my future sent a chill through my heart and a shudder through my body.

Soon after this, I was not allowed to visit any friends who had brothers. I'd protested that most of them were only younger brothers, but that didn't matter to Mr Anderson. His decision had been made. They were free to come to my house but I was never allowed to go to theirs.

This seemed so very unfair both to them and to me and naturally the invitations soon died away. Therese, my friend from swimming, convinced me to join the local youth group made up only of school-age Catholics from Soubirous and De La Salle College (a Catholic boys' school), seen to be a safe place for young men and women to meet while avoiding parental distress over drive-ins and other seemingly seedy places.

This was where I met Michael Banner, a Year 12 boy everyone in my circle thought was quite cute. Not too long after I started going to the club, a night was planned for everyone to visit Toombul Ice Skating Rink and Michael asked if I would like a lift in his car (the front seat, mind you). Adhering to all the rites and rituals required of these young men, he presented himself at my house to ask permission to take me.

Mr Anderson talked to Michael quietly alone in the lounge room while I sat in the kitchen. His request was apparently granted and the outing proceeded, although I do remember thinking at the time that Michael appeared a little cool towards me, unlike other times at youth meetings when we'd gotten on quite well.

I didn't hear from him for almost two weeks after that but I jumped every time the phone rang. Eventually, I dug up the courage to do the unheard of—I phoned him. With my heart in my mouth and hands shaking, I said, 'Hi! Remember me? Have I done something wrong?'

After a slight hesitation, he asked me, 'Did your father tell you what he said to me on the skating night?'

My heart sank. He hadn't, of course.

'No,' I said. 'And by the way, he's not my father. But tell me.'

'Well, he said that I was to stay away from you after that night and if I ever contacted you again, I would be hearing from his solicitor. Look, I don't know what the problem is, but my Dad will kill me if I get in any sort of trouble. I'm sorry.'

Michael had nothing to do with me from then on and my heart broke for the first time. I remember gulping to stop myself from crying.

Needless to say, my chances of having a boyfriend were destroyed at the same time as the visits to the weekly youth club ended.

Mr Anderson's interest in me was becoming an ever-worsening situation.

He began sporting bright, shiny satin shirts of luminous greens and purples with snug-fitting chequered pants as well as a new toupee that didn't quite match his own hair colour (however little there was left). Sometimes his 'rug' slid sideways during sudden turns of his head, leaving it balancing precariously on his smooth dome.

When he started showing favouritism towards me over Adam with little gifts of a chocolate bar or a book brought home from work, I knew this to be a bad sign and started to refuse the gifts, eventually quite rudely, to get the point across to him. I wanted no part of it.

I hated him with a passion and avoided him constantly so there would be no conflict. Then, to my horror, Mrs Anderson commenced working at the local drive-in theatre five nights a week, leaving me alone to deal with him.

Coming into the bathroom to wash me became his next ploy. A locked door finished that approach but started him insisting that I sit on his lap where he would run his hand up my leg, asking me when I would be his 'big girl' or saying, 'All of this is mine. You belong to me. No-one wants you, but I do.' He said he would show me how to please him and show my gratitude. I hated the feel of his cold hands on my legs but I clenched my teeth together and sat as still as I could. In my mind, I floated above the ground. Above whatever was happening below. I flew through the windows out into the night, under the stars. I wasn't *there*.

The sleeping arrangements changed as well at this time with Adam, then aged seven, sleeping every night with Mrs Anderson, and Mr Anderson moving into Adam's room.

One night when Mrs Anderson was at work, I'd only just gone to sleep when I was woken again by the feel of a hand touching my body. Mr Anderson was lying in bed with me. No words can explain the horror I felt as his clammy hands moved all over me. I flung back the covers and slapped his hands away hysterically, then ran to the corner and stood screaming at him, 'Get out! Get out!'

I felt sick to my stomach but I was too scared to go to the toilet. I knew I was crying because my hair was damp from tears, but I wasn't making any noise.

As I sat in the corner curled into a ball, I retreated to my dreams for the first time. I imagined myself walking barefoot along a beach. I could smell fish and seaweed, and salt in the air. No-one else was on the beach with me and I stood with my feet in the water while my toes dug deep in the wet sand, which felt like sugar beneath my feet. The water receded with a dragging feeling, almost overbalancing me and then splashing up my legs as it came back in again. It was hypnotising. I felt calm and at peace as the breeze blew my hair around my face and my dress hugged my body and legs. I sat down on the sand and hunched over my up-drawn knees, squinting at the ocean as the sun blazed down on me. I scooped sand up in my hand and felt the coarse grains filter through my fingers. I could see white-topped waves crashing on the beach, their regular rhythm merging with the sound of the seagulls that flew in circles, wheeling and crying, flapping their wings. So peaceful.

I remember a sound from outside my door suddenly disturbed me and the image disappeared. I was back in my nightmare again.

I ran and locked my bedroom door and did so every night from then on. I became a very light sleeper, jumping at the occasional scrape of a tree limb against the window or the sound of the house timbers settling, listening to the tap dripping and the clock ticking.

If I'd been asked to draw a picture of my world, it would have been black. The innocence that every child deserves was lost to me forever.

The building blocks of my life had already been laid at previous foster homes. This attention from Mr Anderson was nothing new. Sadly, he had taken these building blocks and added to them in ways that a thirteen-year-old girl should never have to experience. That last visit into my bedroom, after everything else, was the straw that broke the camel's back. I'd had enough. The nightly insistence I sit on his lap so that he could touch and feel me would never happen again, I vowed.

His anger must have gotten the better of him because physical beatings started soon after, supposedly as punishment for my being rude and ungrateful. The first time his hand came into contact with my face, my vision exploded with light then blurred, and the sound of bees buzzing in my head filled the air as I leant against the kitchen wall.

Jennifer had said to go to her straight away if anything happened. If I had, I'd have been there every week. The only way for me to cope with this new ordeal was to try to block it out of my mind, putting an imaginary brick wall around myself. I learnt not to show any feelings or emotions—that would have been a sign of weakness. I didn't want him to see how much I was hurting inside.

My life was a chaotic mix of very conflicting emotions. While I felt vulnerable and desperately wanted someone—anyone—to help me, I just couldn't ask for that help. No-one would believe me. My frustration turned into an almost uncontrollable anger: anger at my life, anger with Mr Anderson and fury at Mrs Anderson.

Surely she knew what was happening. She must have seen the bruises and cut lips. Why did she ignore them? Did she know what he was doing? Did she just choose to ignore it? Why? They had adopted other girls before me and two had never been heard of again—could this be the reason? Surely that was too much of a coincidence. Why did she keep allowing this to happen? Didn't she know that by ignoring him, she was giving him permission to continue? She was actually condoning his behaviour.

I hated her as much as I hated him. She was no better than he was.

Only that week at school, I had read that on the way to his execution, Sir Thomas More had said to Henry VIII, 'Silence is consent.' Now I knew what he meant.

Jennifer's words came back to haunt me. Had this happened to her as well? I wanted to tell her what was happening but shame stopped me and even if I did tell her, wouldn't Mr Anderson simply deny it? After all, it was my word against his, and I was just a kid.

Looking back now, I realise that at fifty-five years old, Mrs Anderson couldn't have started a new life even if she had wanted to. It was easier for her to turn a blind eye to everything and have her life stay as it was. In those days, women believed that they needed a man in their lives. Nowadays, women can go anywhere and find a job far more easily than a man can. We can waitress or do clerical work—the options are endless. But it was certainly different then. A woman needed a man, especially at Mrs Anderson's age. So it was easier for her to go along with what was happening. This weak man was probably better than no man at all. Even though he was a failure at everything in his life, a loser, he was better than nothing.

This weak woman's choice to ignore what was happening condemned me to a life of isolation and aloneness. Outwardly, I looked like a sullen adolescent, but inside, I was screaming.

After an incident one night that left me with a broken finger and a swollen, bruised cheek—I was certainly getting used to the coppery taste of blood in my mouth—I asked for something that I never thought I'd want . . . I asked to be sent back to Nazareth House. I was thirteen now and the prospect of returning to life at the orphanage was better by far than staying with the Andersons.

I remember glancing at the kitchen table, looking for

something to hit him with. *Don't worry about what happens. You can do it. Grab the plate. Do it.*

I could actually see myself hitting him. *He might hit me harder. He might even kill me,* I remember thinking. *So what? You feel dead already.* I felt like there were two people inside me having this conversation: one strong, one weak. But for all my bravado, in reality, I was really only a scared little thirteen year old. My hands began to shake as I heard Mr Anderson say, 'You asked for it. You know that, don't you?' It was only then I realised that he was slightly scared himself, and my fear of him subsided a little.

'No-one wants you back at Nazareth House,' he said. 'No-one even wants to see you again and by the way, you'll never see your sister Robyn either.'

His eyes were fixed on me.

My strength vanished with that one sentence. I remember feeling frozen. *A sister? I don't remember any sister! It simply couldn't be true. This must be just another way to hurt me.*

Still, it stayed in the back of my mind.

Robyn was an Irish name. If he was lying, why hadn't he chosen a name like Mary or something equally as common? Why Robyn?

By then, a huge argument had erupted. It was then I was told that at my father's request, an appointment had been made for me to see him in a fortnight's time.

In retrospect, this appointment was probably the reason for all the tension that resulted in the fight that night. Mr Anderson was more than likely worried that I'd tell Dad what had been happening.

The remark about a sister was pushed to the back of my mind with this wonderful news—I was ecstatic. It had been well over a year since I'd last seen my father and I dreamt of begging him to take me with him—anywhere, as long as I was with him. Everything would be all right again. I would look after him and we would be together, just him and me. For the first time in over a year, I went to bed happy.

When I woke up, my face was stiff and for the next few days I could hardly see out of my eye. No-one seemed to acknowledge what had happened except that my finger was taped up and I was told not to go to school. For the next five days, I simply sat in my room and looked out of the window at the view of Mrs Cooper's garden from the back of our house. Solitude became a friend that I welcomed at this time.

Again I went to my beach.

The next two weeks dragged as I waited impatiently for the day to arrive.

The June holidays had come and gone and it was now well into July. Like any thirteen year old anticipating a happy event, I was dressed and waiting hours before we left on that cold, windy winter's morning.

The appointment was for midday, but by 11.30 we were there in the waiting room, my enthusiasm bringing smiles even to Mrs Anderson.

Midday came and went.

One o'clock, then two o'clock and three o'clock.

As the clock ticked on, my worst fears crept over me like a dark shadow. He wasn't coming at all.

I was totally shattered.

What could have been so important that it kept him from showing up to see me? I remember thinking.

Crying all the way home, I eventually sobbed, 'Why didn't he turn up?'

The vision of Mr Anderson turning around in the passenger side of the front seat will always stay with me. His explanation was delivered like a slap in the face: 'Your father was drunk,' he said brutally.

I was filled with anger and bitterness at being betrayed by

my father, and stormed into my room refusing dinner and any consolation. I just wanted to be left alone.

So there I stayed, alone, with an aching heart and a vow never to let anyone hurt me ever again.

The next year passed uneventfully. I closed myself away from everyone, only going to school during the week and staying in my room when I was at home. It was the only way I could function.

Every Sunday, Mr Anderson, smiling and nodding to other parishioners, would still take Adam and me to church, displaying us in our very best outfits for everyone to see. I could barely keep the contempt from showing on my face.

I gave up smiling and I never prayed any more. Praying was like wishing, and wishes never came true.

I was told that the Andersons had applied on several occasions over the previous two years to adopt me but my father had refused to sign any such papers. This provided little consolation because now, almost twelve months after the failed meeting, I was told that my adoption papers had been duly signed and were ready for my signature.

At fourteen years of age and in Year 9 at school, I couldn't understand why the Andersons even bothered any more. I certainly wasn't the loving daughter they supposedly wanted when they decided to take me out of Nazareth House. I didn't love them, and I gave them very little to love.

Still, this was the final rejection. The last straw.

My mother was always drunk and had never even bothered to visit me in the home and my father couldn't even stay sober long enough to see me. Now after another year, he was getting rid of me just like everyone else had. So, gritting my teeth and snatching the pen, I signed the papers.

I had a plan in mind. I would finish school at the end of Year 10 and start work, doing anything. A job came up for a junior at a local bank, making coffee and doing menial jobs, so I took it while waiting for the results of a Public Service exam that I had sat.

My first paycheque bought me two suitcases; my second was set aside for bond money for a flat. At age fifteen, with almost $100 in the bank and a letter of acceptance from the Public Service, I waited until the Andersons were out one Saturday morning before reading the section in the paper advertising 'flats to rent'. After phoning and accepting one sight unseen, I packed my bags and left a note saying only, 'Goodbye.'

Three years of fighting off the bastard was enough.

As I stepped out of the house with suitcases in hand and walked towards the cab I'd called, I glanced towards the heavens, silently asking, *So, what's next? Another flood? A plague of locusts? Do your worst, I don't care. I'm free!*

I could see a light at the end of the tunnel. I only hoped it wasn't a train coming straight at me.

CHAPTER 7

✛

Miniskirts and Wedge Shoes

'Hello?'

'Hi, Rob. It's me,' I started. 'Tony said you called while I was out.'

'Hi. Yeah. Look, a woman by the name of Sandra Stewart called me trying to contact you. For some reason, she thinks she's your sister.'

Trying to be firm but not sound rude, I told him, 'Rob, you know that can't be true.' We'd been married twelve years and he knew all about my past. 'I'm really not up to this right now. I'm tired, and I'm pretty sure she's got her wires crossed somewhere. I've never heard of her and I really don't feel like talking to anyone at the moment.' *It's just not possible, I thought.* 'Thanks for not giving out my number—could you do me a favour and call her back and say something to get rid of her? I've just never heard of a Sandra Stewart.'

'She said you might feel like this,' he said a little tentatively, 'but she also said you may not know her as Sandra, but possibly as Robyn.'

I started shaking, shivering on this warm summer night. I

could feel perspiration popping out on my top lip but I also felt cold and clammy.

I couldn't believe this!

'She said she was thirty-eight and had been adopted at birth,' he continued. 'Because her adoptive parents are both dead now, she decided to try and find her birth parents. When she received her original birth certificate, she found out that her parents' names were Ernest Joseph Gourgaud and Merle Rose Mooney and that she had a sister by the name of Patricia Gourgaud, aged four.'

I didn't need to hear any more.

'Oh my God,' I said irreverently. 'Oh my God!' *It was true??* 'Have you got the number?'

I wrote the telephone number on a piece of paper, thanked him and shakily sat down. I was nervous, confused, excited and scared all at once.

After all these years, was it possible? How the hell could this be happening? This was such a total contradiction to the years that followed my walk-out from the Andersons to start my new life.

My new flat hadn't been exactly what I'd imagined, but it was in a good position and only a twenty-minute bus ride, after a thirty-minute walk, to work. I put up with the smell of cooking food wafting over day and night from the take-away restaurant across the road because in the same block there was a laundromat as well as a corner store that sold bread, milk, tea, coffee, papers and the sort of things people forget when they do their weekly shopping. This shop was ideal for me. I needed very little to survive.

The flat contained two rooms: a kitchen with only a fridge, gas cooktop, one square table and two chairs as hard as church pews; and, through a set of French doors, a bedroom with only a single bed and a wardrobe. An uncurtained window let in some light, filtered through the trees, but not enough to warm up the cold linoleum floor in winter. The bathroom used by all residents was at the end of a hallway at the back of the house. It was all very spartan, but as much as I could afford now that I was a lowly Clerical Assistant Grade 1 working for the Commonwealth Government. There were no pictures on the walls, no knick-knacks to dust, no vases of coloured glass or souvenir ashtrays to accidentally knock over.

I saw myself standing in the dirt in front of the 'ladder to success'—not even on the first rung yet—but single-minded, concentrating only on my job and putting everything else out of my mind. But at least I had control of my own life and no-one would demand any explanation from me that I might not be ready to give.

This was to be my home for the next three years. I'd heard people referring to themselves as poor and I guess that was me too in my day-to-day struggle to survive. But the alternative didn't bear thinking about.

What I remember most about those years were the simple things. The first meal I ever bought myself. The immense happiness of being able to cross the road from my flat to the take-away, buying the food and bringing it home to eat. Bought with my own money. Eaten in my own flat. No-one could take this away from me. All I wanted was stability and peace. My early years made me afraid of hoping for contentment. Sure, I was lonely again, but in comparison to what I had come from, things seemed brighter. I needed very little money. I lived simply.

The nights were blissful. I could lie in bed and hear the swish of cars driving past, the distant music of a radio playing or sometimes the soft patter of rain on the roof. No more did I have to lie awake, alert to any sound in the night or listening for quiet footsteps at my door. For so many years, I'd wandered between reality and fantasy but now, to my surprise, some degree of contentment and purpose had emerged.

In my whole life, I'd never done anything remarkable or looked at myself seriously. Never valued myself enough. I'd always been very private, almost apologetic. A skittish, shy creature. Getting through school, learning, growing up. I'd been barely hanging on. But I knew there had once been a passion inside me. A fire burning. There was still an ember glowing, just waiting to be fanned. Like most of the kids at the home, I thought of myself as just an accident. But something made me want to stand up and be counted. I didn't want my life to be insignificant. I wanted to shout out, 'Hey, I'm a nice person and I am worthwhile.'

As it turned out, the Commonwealth Government Public Service sent me to do clerical work at a hospital. Greenslopes Repatriation Hospital. The irony of the situation did not escape me.

At the beginning, I kept to myself, not making friends and not caring. I didn't want or need anyone. I felt empty inside. I had an image of myself. A dead leaf drifting in the wind, devoid of emotion. All I wanted was to work and to be left alone.

Little things scared me. Getting on a bus that went in the wrong direction. Being even one minute late for work. Sometimes I would cry for no reason at all. I was frightened by small noises. Suspicious and afraid of strangers. I was always nervous. 'You're on your own,' I repeated to myself. 'You're on your own.'

After the obligatory six months in the file room, I found myself promoted to Ward Secretary in Ward 12/13, the Chest Ward—the exact ward I had played outside years ago while visiting my father.

I remember looking around the grounds, reliving the nights sitting on the grass with the toads. Those times had seemed so happy and I remembered with a heavy heart all the hugs and kisses my father had given me then.

Why had he deserted me? What had I done to make him not want me any more, just like my mother?

I remembered how tall he seemed to me and how blue his eyes were, the concave part of his back where his left lung had been removed and the hat he always wore whenever he had come to visit me.

God, I'd loved him so much.

To this day, his resemblance to Humphrey Bogart, with his hat perched jauntily on his head, sends a sharp pang through my heart.

Even though my life was vastly different now, my inbuilt reticence made it difficult for me to make friends, although people had tried. At first, no-one spoke to me. That was all right; I didn't know what to say anyway. Eventually, they started to ask questions, wanting to know about me. But I couldn't open up and tell anyone about my life. Beside the fact I thought that no-one would have believed me, I didn't want anyone's pity or sympathy. I was trying to move on from all of that. So I kept to myself. My recovery was slow and I sometimes thought it would never be complete.

I was asked out occasionally in the beginning but the offers soon stopped after I overheard a young man, who'd already asked me out and been refused, commenting to another that I was a 'cold fish'. His insult brought a little pain to the pit of my stomach and a lump to my throat. My pride had felt a twinge of hurt, but I did nothing. I couldn't stand anyone touching me anyway, not even brushing past me in the corridor.

I tried imagining what it would feel like to be normal. I would walk down the hospital corridors and people would stop and smile and ask, 'How are you, Trish?' and really mean it. They would ask me to go out in their group to dinner or someone's house, and be so pleased when I said yes. I would be liked and sought after as their friend.

They were lovely dreams. In reality all I could manage was a quick nod, and then I would drop my head and walk on silently.

I feared closeness. My fear of men almost had me believing I had a vocation to be a nun. So I worked and saved my money, choosing not to spend anything on my small flat, instead buying much-needed clothes.

For the first time, I could buy what I wanted. Probably a little foolishly, I followed the latest trends of the early 1970s and bought short dresses, high wedge shoes. I actually bought many bad outfits. And I had my hair done.

Up until then, my hair had been in no particular style, just pulled back into the ponytail that I'd always wanted. It hung life-lessly down to my shoulders and the overall result hadn't been what I'd imagined. I decided to have my hair cut into a fashionable Farrah Fawcett style and I almost didn't know the new person who emerged. After coming home from the hairdressers, I looked in the mirror and asked, 'Is this person me? Is it really me?' My hair was now soft and feathered around my face after the light perm I'd had. My nose was a little too large for my liking. Green eyes that had regained a little of their long-forgotten sparkle although there was still fear and disquiet in their depths. Like a deer caught in the head-lights, I was held there by my own gaze, wondering if I would ever find someone who would love, understand and accept me.

On reflection, the new clothes that I bought were totally unsuitable for my job as the Ward Secretary of a heart and chest ward. But no-one said anything to me. I can still remember clomping along the wooden verandah in my miniskirt and plat-form shoes, oblivious to everyone staring at me. I must have been regarded more as a health risk than a help to the poor old gentlemen who had been sent to Greenslopes to recuperate.

This was my awakening period. My transformation, if you want. I began to feel I was a worthwhile person, to believe it for the first time in my life. And bad memories started to fade as my life opened up for me. It seemed so inconceivable, so impossible that this could happen. But it did.

I loved my job. I loved everything about it. The independence, the security—and especially being a part of a group and not alone any more. I'd discovered that if I wanted to talk to someone, I could. If I needed to be alone, that was no trouble either. I couldn't remember being happier.

When I'd arrived at Nazareth House, I became someone else. Possibly not even some*one* else; a group of people in one body. I'd changed my personality so many times in the hope of being wanted, I didn't know who I was any more. 'Would the real Patricia Gourgaud please stand up?'

I was starting to find out who I was.

As time went on, I grew more confident in myself and I started to change again. The fire of my youth returned and I could now say 'No' to things that I had given in to for so many years. I was able to experience everything at my own pace. I thawed and learnt how to interact with other people while I grew and developed as a person. I made a few friends at work, and although I still preferred my own company, I made one important friendship that has lasted for over twenty years to this day.

David was a hospital orderly working to pay for flying lessons when we met. His job was to bring patients down from the wards to have their X-rays taken. By that time, I'd had a promotion to Clerical Assistant Grade 3 and was working in the X-ray Department. David had been one of my first friends, one I needed desperately, at Greenslopes Hospital and we'd clicked immediately. He made me—and everyone—laugh. That was his great gift. And he liked me just for myself—no ulterior motives. I even introduced him to a girl who worked with me and he eventually married her.

I was eighteen when I met Rob. My first boyfriend. I guess I liked him enough, but trust? That would maybe come later, I thought. He was very charming and I was very needy. I needed to be wanted and loved so desperately. Doesn't everyone? When I first started to date him, I thought it would never come to anything serious. I was too short, reserved, and felt inadequate for stupid reasons. Breasts not big enough, nose too big. Maybe you can imagine how I felt? But six months later, I jumped at the first marriage offer made to me. I was far too young, but I believed I had found love, when really I only needed to be loved. I remember feeling so grateful. He was so wonderful and good-looking, and he wanted me. ME. My own mother hadn't, why would anyone else?

I'd never eaten in an outdoor restaurant or been away on a holiday. I'd never slept with a man. I did all three on my wedding night.

After my marriage, the next few years of my life seemed fairly normal. My previous life had been hard and chaotic. Now I had to work at making my new life one that was full of peace and happiness.

Between the two of us, we had enough money saved for a deposit on a small house, in an average suburb—paying off a mortgage like so many other young couples. The only furniture we could afford was a double bed, a fridge, two beanbags, and a small black and white portable television sitting on a coffee table. All washing had to be either done by hand or up at the local laundromat. But we were happy. We both had jobs and life seemed pretty sweet. Over the next few years we saved for other items of furniture and my husband's family helped us as much as they could. These things were all new for me. I moved in a daze of happiness.

My husband's family were European and as was the custom in many Mediterranean families, the women's needs seemed to take a back seat to the men's wishes. It appeared that the women's sole purpose in life was to look after the men, almost as though the men were a different species from them. I began to feel like I was back at the Andersons' again. This virtual subservience didn't sit very well with my newfound independence, and arguments popped up out of the blue more and more frequently. But still I was love-struck.

Eventually, after many hints from my husband's parents, we decided to try for a family of our own. While I looked forward to the prospect of motherhood, I was also terrified by it. I would be totally responsible for a little baby. Totally. I hadn't so much as held a baby, let alone fed or changed one. I knew I could depend on my mother-in-law for help but I couldn't rely on her for everything.

After five years of marriage and one miscarriage along the way, I finally fell pregnant again. I hadn't realised it would take me so long. Here I was trying desperately to have a baby, while fifteen-year-old girls were having sex in the back of cars for the first time and falling pregnant straight away. Where was the logic or fairness in that?

Finally on Friday July 13th 1979 my eight-pound baby boy was born, with bruises down one side of his face and his nose pushed out of shape from the difficult birth. I named him Mark. He was the most beautiful baby I had ever seen in my life, and he was mine.

He slept well and rarely cried, and I found myself sitting for hours with him asleep on my chest, just so I could hold him longer. His early dark hair fell out at three months to leave him totally bald but very soon after, a fine growth of almost white hair started to grow on his head.

I knew his colouring came from me (his father was dark haired with an olive complexion) but I had no idea where our fair hair came from. Both my mother and father had almost black hair.

He never crawled but went straight to running at ten

months old. How had my mother given me up after going through all the happiness of watching a baby grow?

Before I knew it, Mark was three years old and I was pregnant again.

When a second boy arrived, my husband's family decided amongst themselves that this one would have a family name. An old uncle in Yugoslavia was called Tony so that would be the new baby's name.

Again, this baby was perfect but he was so different from Mark it was hard to believe that they were brothers. Mark still had his white-blond hair, light brown eyes and a gorgeous, mischievous grin while Tony had almost black hair, my green eyes and a 'melt your heart' smile.

I had stopped full-time work after the birth of my first child in order to raise my small family, working only part-time as a function hostess with a wine distributor until falling pregnant with my second son.

Things at home were starting to be more and more strained as we found it increasingly difficult to maintain our family on a single wage. When Tony was one year old, I resumed part-time work as a waitress with Pizza Hut, until after four years I felt my family could cope with my working full time.

Over the following three years, I rose through the ranks by working hard and completing a management course, until I was managing a restaurant on my own. I loved this job. The hours were long and I found myself working most nights until midnight, oblivious to the effect it was having on my family.

With both of my boys still in primary school, the reality of my commitment to work was brought home to me one night, when after awaking from a nightmare, my youngest son called out for his father instead of me. I realised then that I had come full circle and had put my children in the same position I had been in when I was a child. I had always said that I would be 'there' for my children but I had turned into a lousy mother, just like my own.

Mum (aged nineteen) and a friend at Uncle Terry and Aunt Laurel's
wedding, about 1945.

Nanna Mooney, Mum and Uncle Terry, about 1945.

Nanna Mooney, Aunt Laurel and Mum. (The children are Aunt Laurel's two oldest—my cousins.)

Mum and me—May 1955.

Dad—Tobruk (in the Second World War) 1942.

Pop on the left and Dad on the right.

Me aged eighteen.

Mark aged four.

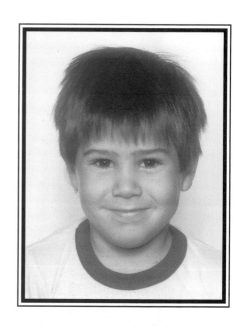

Tony aged four.

Above: Sandra and me as we look today.

Right: My wedding day— Mark on the right, Tony on the left. PHOTO: Peter Wanny

Below: David and me on our wedding day—Valentine's Day, 1999. PHOTO: Peter Wanny

Right: General Gaspar Gourgaud.

Below: Our honeymoon in Paris. The picture says it all.

I could try to justify my reasons for working most nights: I was unskilled with little education, I was doing it for my family, we needed the money—all true—but the result was still the same, I had put myself ahead of them and was unknowingly pushing them away. In fifty years' time, the type of car we drove or the amount of money in the bank wouldn't matter. But it would matter to my children that I was with them while they were growing up.

I resigned from my job the next day.

I was no longer the unassuming, cowering wife who gave in to all arguments just to keep the peace, and was strong enough to stand up for myself and what I believed in. Possibly because of this change, together with the long-term effects of too many nights working while my husband stayed at home minding the children, Rob and I finally agreed our marriage was over. His family could rely on him for anything. Not me. Marriage at eighteen had seemed right at the time but we had definitely been too young; neither of us had had the chance to experience life before settling down with a family. In the early days, my inno-cence had saved me. But now, I was a totally different person.

Now after having dropped ten kilos over the years, I would not have to endure the bewildering hurt as Rob slapped food out of my hands. I remember asking him once why he'd done such a thing. 'You don't want to be fat, do you?' he'd said. I was only forty-seven kilos at the time. Then he'd added, 'I only want to be proud of you.' How do you forgive something like that? His was a handsome gene pool but a shallow one.

He moved out. The conditions were not negotiable.

CHAPTER 8

✣

Darwin's First Rule

I wonder how many of us stop to take stock of our lives. Could I have done other things? With life's endless choices, I sometimes wondered what it would have been like if I'd taken a different fork in the road.

When I'd left the Andersons, I felt that I had no choice but to do what I did, but what if I'd persevered a while longer, stayed at school and done something with my life? In my youth, I'd often dreamt of becoming an archaeologist and I could almost see myself in an Egyptian tomb, or an Aztec ruin, digging in the hot sun and feeling I was doing something worthwhile.

But in the few weeks since Rob and I had separated, I thought about this and knew that my Vinnies' dresses were unsuitable for the architectural digs I'd dreamt of! Also, the responsibility of raising my children meant that those early choices were definitely no longer available to me.

I had two beautiful boys, my treasures, whom I would die for if I had to and whom I would never give up, no matter what the situation or circumstances. My mother had walked out and left me like I was some unwanted piece of trash. I would never, could never, do that to my boys. I adored them. But still I wondered.

I started thinking more and more about my mother and the reasons why she gave me up and I realised that I could think about her differently now that I was a mother myself. It couldn't have been easy for her to do such a totally unnatural thing, unless, of course, she felt she had no other choice. My mother had been an alcoholic and today alcoholism is regarded as a disease. It changes people and makes them into total strangers doing things they wouldn't normally do. I knew that. But what had put her onto that path?

I started reading books and articles written by psychologists on early childhood and was amazed at some of the insights they offered. A Dr Robertiello said that most girls are products of their mother's love, whether the mother is aloof or smothering. What we must do is break down the specific components of our mother's love—analyse exactly the ways she did not love us but also the ways in which she did. Did your mother give you a kind of basic security—a structure of stability, shelter, nurturing? Did she give you admiration—a genuine feeling that you were worth plenty in your own right? Did she give you warmth and physical affection, cuddles, hold and kiss you? Did she really care what happened to you and accept you—my daughter, right or wrong? These are some of the components of real love. When a tiny child doesn't get that kind of satisfying affection and love, they do not evolve emotionally. They grow older but part of them is still looking for that closeness and when they find it, they fear it will soon be taken away.

Considering this and knowing it applied to me and possibly to my mother, I tried to put myself in my mother's place as well: loving and living with a married man, a small child in tow and Nanna Mooney's cool aloofness. I actually started feeling sorry for her. I remembered Nanna Mooney's scowling face and wondered if that had been reserved for me or if my mother had lived her childhood seeing it as well. I had no idea.

Because of my youth, she and I were never able to talk about our feelings. I could have come to terms with her angers, disillusionments and other emotions, if I'd been older. I would have understood that while my mother loved me, other emotions impaired that love. Instead, I was left feeling that I had caused the problems at home.

How lonely she must have been at times, with no-one to turn to. I myself remembered the emptiness of being alone. I knew that being loved and wanted was what I needed more than anything. She was no different to me in that respect.

The doctor's theory was that the deprivation of love stamps a woman for life. Such women have missed something vital from their mothers, and they grow guarded and distrustful. Even as their husbands and lovers tell them that they love them, these women still believe that they will leave and reject them. They marry the first man who asks; they take a civil service job instead of a more demanding career and never believe in themselves. They work in bursts until, having achieved success, they look around and say, 'What does it all mean?' These 'impoverished infants' are still emotionally impoverished as adults despite their worldly success.

Every one of these traits was mine.

I'd often wondered that if I was as strong as I thought I had become, why was I haunted with fear that I wasn't good enough? All my triumphs meant little to me as I endeavoured to do better and better again. I strove to be a winner, but my idea of a winner was someone perfect and, as we all know, none of us is perfect. I had been good at schoolwork and sports, liked by people after I'd come out of my shell and I had succeeded in my working life, but negative feelings had still overshadowed all my accomplishments.

Once again after all these years, I found myself, not alone (I still had my boys), but lonely. Looking at the whole picture of my life, I knew something was missing. At thirty-five years of age, I decided I would try to find my parents.

'Children's Services' is a government department that deals solely in the placement and subsequent care of adopted and fostered children. It maintains records and files on every one of these people.

After numerous letters and lengthy phone calls, during which I was transferred from section to section, I was informed that both of my parents had been deceased for a number of years, my father at age forty-nine and my mother at forty-six. This was a bitter disappointment and one I hadn't even anticipated. It seemed that I had no family to find. Then, for some reason, I suddenly remembered Mr Anderson's spiteful statement about a sister.

I would rather have walked over hot coals than contact Nazareth House, but seeing no other way, I rang, hoping they would have some useful information. As I explained to the secretary what I wanted, she said, 'You would have been here when Sister Philomena was in charge. How wonderful. She's here right now.'

Before I could scream out NO!!!! the familiar Irish brogue was on the other end of the line with a 'Hello, Patricia.'

She remembers me? I recall thinking. *Had I been that unforgettable?*

I felt like I was ten years old and in trouble again. My legs turned to jelly and my hands started sweating as I shakily sat down and stammered my way through my prepared dialogue. With my eyes closed tightly and a pulse pounding in my throat, I repeated what I had told the secretary.

'Hello, Sister. I'm sorry to bother you, but I was wondering if you remember from my records if I had a sister. I was told by my last foster parents that I had one, and I really would like to try and find her.'

After a hesitation, I heard the sorrow in her voice as she said, 'No, Patricia. There was never anything in your file and no mention of a sister. I am truly sorry.'

There was a small silence and then she said, 'What are you doing with your life, dear? Are you married?'

'Yes, Sister. I've got two boys as well,' I replied.

'Oh, that's lovely, dear. And you're happy?'

'Yes, Sister. Everything is fine,' I lied.

We chatted for a few minutes, talking about my children and what I was now doing with my life.

I finished my call to Sister Philomena feeling drained, empty and terribly disappointed. I hadn't told her that I was now divorced and hadn't been to church since I was fifteen, or that it was hard for me to accept the theory of an 'all-loving, all-giving God' who watched over us, when He had been decidedly absent in my life up to now.

I didn't tell her that I couldn't see why not attending church was a 'mortal sin' for all Catholics, when prayers could be said equally as well at home. The concept that I would go to 'hell' for this, no matter how good a person I was, left me feeling very sceptical. I believed then, as I do now, that the main thing is how good a person you are—not how many times you go to church. Praying can be done anywhere and at any time.

In my life, I had seen enough to turn me completely against the regimented religion that Sister Philomena represented. I'd known people who had gone to church regularly but who had left their religion inside that church when they went home.

After talking to her for that little while, I'd started seeing her through the eyes of an adult and not as a child. I started to wonder, *Could I have been wrong about her all these years?*

It only occurred to me then that the nuns had probably done the best they could with the resources that were available.

Although I'd never disagreed with the basic premise that discipline was necessary, the extent of that discipline, and the methods used, were different matters.

Still, the nuns were untrained, trying to do a difficult job and more than likely had been thrown into their situation the same way the children were. It was like telling a group of carpenters that they were now brain surgeons. The nuns had possibly never wanted children of their own, joining the convent to embrace religion, and there they were, responsible for fifty or more children as a part of their daily life.

They were segregated, imposed with values and responsibilities that are not part of a normal life, and had to learn to suppress normal desires and needs that conflicted with their newly chosen path. When I actually thought about it, the worst emotional scars of my childhood did not come from these institutions but from other individuals whose care I was put in. Some of these people were wrongly assumed to be virtuous purely because of their religious background, making those foster homes an even worse nightmare than what I had been taken away from.

Anger slowly surfaced again as I remembered Mr Anderson's lie told to hurt me as a child. I felt like I had been running around in circles looking for something that just wasn't there. Still, I'd given it my best shot and pursued all avenues I could think of.

I decided that from then on, Darwin's rule that the fittest will survive was going to apply to me. Life keeps going on. I saw myself as just an ordinary person who, having been tested, had to ask myself, 'Will I crumble, give up and fall down in a heap, or will I rise up out of these circumstances?' I could sit on my backside and wonder why all of this had happened to me or I could just get on with things. From the rubble of my life, I would survive. I was damn sure I would.

After this mental shake-up, I decided I'd had enough time to think things over. It was time to go out and earn some money again, not throw my arms up in the air in defeat. Nothing lasts forever and I knew this bad patch would pass too. After all, life is all about moving on, and change can occur at random and sometimes at unpredictable intervals. This was my chance to prove it.

I worked at several places over the next few years until I eventually scraped enough money together to buy and run a small coffee shop. Running the shop meant I could control the hours I spent working, enabling me to be with my boys every afternoon and evening. I needed my children as much as they needed me.

I couldn't count on anyone but myself but, on the other hand, I didn't have to live up to anyone else's expectations.

CHAPTER 9

✦

All I'd Really Wanted

'Are you all right, Mum?' Tony had turned around on the lounge and was looking at me.

'You were right, Tony,' I said, not quite believing it myself. 'Your father just had a phone call from a woman who says she's my sister. How about that?' I said in a tremulous voice.

Both boys looked at me in amazement. The only comment was from Mark. 'Cool.'

It took my shaking fingers three attempts to dial the correct number, but after a single ring a woman's voice answered, 'Hello?'

'Sandra Stewart?' I almost whispered.

'Yes,' she said tentatively.

Seconds ticked by in absolute silence as I realised that I hadn't even thought of what I was going to say.

'Trish?'

That single word was all I needed to start tears running down my cheeks, and with a lump the size of an orange in my throat all I could croak out was, 'Yes . . . Oh God . . . I'm sorry.'

I sobbed as I said, 'You just don't know how much this means to me.'

'Did you know about me?' she asked, crying just as much as I was. 'Is it really true?'

'Yes, I think it is true. I hope so. I tried to find you years ago, but everyone said that you didn't exist. I can't believe it. Please, you talk, I can't. How did you find me?' That was all I could manage to say.

'God, I don't know where to start. All right. When I was twelve years old, my father told me that I had been adopted. My mother died when I was four years old but my father died only a few months ago.'

She took a deep breath before continuing. Struggling with the emotion in her voice she said, 'I went through all his things and Jill, she's my sister who was adopted as well, found her papers but I couldn't find mine. We looked everywhere but they weren't around. I guess it was then that I decided to try to find my real parents, more particularly, my mother.

'So I rang Children's Services and they sent out a booklet and a form to fill out so I could get my adoption records. They also sent a form that gave me the authority to get my original birth certificate.'

I could hear how hard this was for her, so I simply said, 'Go on. I'm still here.'

'Anyway,' she started, 'these departments take forever to send you anything but eventually I received the authorisation form to take to the Registry Office. I'll never forget that day. I opened the letter and for the first time, I saw my parents' names—but not just that. It said that I had been named Robyn Ann and I had a sister by the name of Patricia Therese Gourgaud who had been four years old when I was adopted.' She sniffled before continuing.

'All I could do was to go outside and cry for ages. When my husband came outside and asked if I was all right, I couldn't even talk. All I'd really wanted was a mother and now I had a sister.'

Sounding a little more comfortable now that she was into familiar territory, she said, 'The next day, I went into the Registry

Office to apply for my original birth certificate from the Births, Deaths and Marriages department. They don't just give it to you over the counter, did you know that?'

'No,' I said. 'I've never had to get one. Go on.'

'Anyway, I went back the next day, which was Friday, to pick it up and sure enough, my birth name was Robyn Ann and your name was listed as a sibling on the certificate. On Sunday night, my husband and I were talking and wondering what nationality Gourgaud was, so we opened the phone book and there were three listings. He said to me, "Why don't you ring?"'

'I was so nervous; I said to him, "No, you ring for me."'

She was talking so fast I had to really concentrate so I didn't miss anything.

'He came back and said, "It's French. Ring them back and see if they know anyone by the name of Patricia. There's only three or four in the book and it's not a common name."'

'So I did. I wasn't sure what to say or how to start the conversation so when a woman answered, I just blurted out, "Hi. My name is Sandra Stewart and my husband just rang up asking about the nationality of your name. I was adopted and I just got my birth certificate and I wanted to know if you know an Ernest Gourgaud?"'

'The first thing she said was, "Is that you, Robyn?"'

Sandra started to cry again but between sniffles she said, 'I couldn't help crying. Someone actually knew who I was. You know, everything was happening so fast.'

She stopped to take another deep breath and collect herself. 'She said her name was Paula and that Ernie was her father. That meant that she was my half-sister. Yours too. Did you know that?'

I had been listening with my mouth open in amazement. I had no idea who Paula was. A half-sister?

'No, I didn't,' I said. 'If she knew about you, did she know about me?'

'Yes, she did. She mentioned something about going to the Exhibition with you when you were just a kid.'

'I remember that,' I jumped in. 'I didn't know she was my sister, though. She was just someone who was there with Dad and me. She was there with her husband, I think. Oh my God. That was Paula? She walked around with us all day and I had no idea who she was.'

'Well, she knows you. Anyway, after getting my birth certificate, I had to go back to the Registry Office to try and find out if you were married and what your name was. Since your name was on my certificate, that was enough proof of identity for me to get your records. They only do searches in five-year slots and they charge you for every slot. So I took a guess and I was right the first time. That was so lucky. The same guy served me again and he went out the back and came back with your married name. He said if I wanted your address, I could find it at the Electoral Office. He was really nice. I've been in there three times and he's served me every time. He knows as much as I do,' she laughed.

'When was this?' I asked, trying to get the time sequence straight in my mind.

'Today. Just today. As soon as I found you on the electoral roll, I ran to the nearest phone in Queen Street Mall and phoned my husband. All I could say was, "I found her! I've really found her!" I was so happy. Earlier tonight, we looked in the phone book but I couldn't find your name, so I tried directory assistance and they said your number was unlisted. There were only a few people with your surname in the book, so I rang the first one. Your husband answered—well, your ex-husband answered. When I asked if he knew you, he just said, "Who's this?"

'I had to go through everything all over again from the start. I finished by telling him my name was Sandra Stewart but he was reluctant to give me your number. When I said that you might know me as Robyn, there was a long silence before he said, "I'm her ex-husband. I'll give Trish a ring and see if she wants to talk to you." I'm so glad you did ring.'

'I just can't believe it. I have to see you. Where do you live?'

'I live at Mt Warren Park, Beenleigh,' she said.

That was only half an hour away from me. But I would have driven to the moon to see her in any case.

Amazed at the closeness of her house, I asked, 'How long have you lived there?'

'I've lived in Brisbane most of my life,' she replied.

Trying not to push too hard, I asked, 'Can I come now? Would you mind if I came right now?'

'Yeah, sure. I don't mind. You know, you can come tomorrow if you want to.' She sounded tentative but that was understandable. I was feeling nervous myself.

'I'd like to come now, if that's all right.' I had to see her. I'd waited for this moment for so long, I didn't want to wait any longer.

She gave me the address and I hung up.

I turned to the boys and said, 'Guys, I'm going to see her now. I'll be back as soon as I can. Don't wait up. I'll tell you all about it tomorrow night.'

I yelled out, 'Bye,' as I grabbed my bag and keys off the table and ran to the front door. My tiredness had totally disappeared.

Unmoved in any way by the night's events, my cat Oscar was as usual still blocking the busiest thoroughfare in the house. As I stepped over him, I said, 'What do you think about that, Ossie? You've got an aunty.'

He barely lifted his head and tried to focus on me with his crossed eyes.

'Don't get too excited, sweetie. It's not good for you,' I said scratching him behind an ear.

And then I was gone.

CHAPTER 10

$\clubsuit$

Dad's Eyes

The inconvenience of nightfall was lost on me as I sped along the freeway.

Is all this really happening? kept echoing over and over in my head. I'd wanted something like this to happen for so long but had basically given up looking. Now it had come out of the blue.

It had been almost seven years since I'd last spoken to Sister Philomena. In all those years, not a day had gone by when I wasn't wishing that she had made a mistake and I did, after all, have a sister.

Since that phone call to Nazareth House, my life had drifted on almost uneventfully, through good times and bad. Sometimes, on bad days, I remembered feelings that I'd held in check for so long.

In those years, there had been one major hiccup, a disastrous relationship too soon after the break-up of my marriage. Although at the time, I'd been in no rush to enter a new relationship, I'd managed to go from one disaster to another, looking for a fairytale ending but instead finding unhappiness. Once again, love had failed me.

The adage, 'When a fox hears a rabbit screaming it comes running, but not to help' could have been written for me, but luckily this rabbit was able to escape from that relationship with only a few scars. I had learnt my lesson and had spent time licking my wounds, becoming stronger because of it.

If it hadn't been for my boys, I would have run away to another state but because of them, I'd decided to stay in Brisbane. I'd lived here all my life. Be damned if I was going to let a man scare me away. I loved the beaches of the Gold Coast to the south and the Sunshine Coast beaches one hour north. I loved the mountains surrounding Brisbane; cool in the summer months with their picturesque waterfalls and bush tracks. I even loved the contradictions of the city, where busy commuters vied for better positions on the freeways and bridges while small boats floated lazily on the river that meandered through its heart. I loved it all.

And now I'd discovered that Sandra had always lived here too. All these years later, it looked like my prayers for a sister had been mysteriously answered.

Can it be true? Is she really my sister or is this just a terrible mistake? After everything that has happened, what if she doesn't like me or we don't get along?

This was my old insecurity from my childhood raising its ugly head again. The echoes of my youth.

I was jerked back to reality by an oncoming car's high beam and realised I was going way too fast. My thoughts had taken over and I hadn't been concentrating on my driving at all. The turn-off was just ahead of me and I indicated and moved into the left lane.

I'd better slow down and get there in one piece, I thought. *I'm almost there.*

Two minutes later, I pulled up in front of her house. As I walked up the path and knocked on the door, my hands were shaking and my stomach was doing somersaults.

Please, God, I prayed. *If you're really up there, please make it be true.* It was the first time in twenty-five years I'd said a prayer of any sort. I'd become a closet Catholic—no longer a churchgoer but talking to a God I wasn't sure even existed.

A pretty blonde woman greeted me at the door and all my doubts disappeared.

Those beautiful blue eyes! It was like looking at Dad's eyes! I just stood there staring at her. She was about my height and build, with shoulder-length hair. Her high cheekbones accentuated the largeness of her blue eyes. I could see the resemblance between us immediately. I felt choked with emotion as the reality of what was happening sank in.

We hugged a little bashfully, and she said, 'Come in.'

I followed her into the kitchen where a man was standing beside a table. 'This is Farouk,' she said to me.

He leant over and kissed me on the cheek and said, 'I hope you don't mind having an Egyptian as a brother-in-law.'

I smiled as I shook my head.

'Would you like a drink? Coffee? Beer?' he asked.

'A beer would be great,' I said. My throat was dry and my tongue felt like it was stuck to the roof of my mouth.

I sat down and looked at the woman who was my little sister. I just couldn't take my eyes off her. She was absolutely gorgeous.

As I sat holding her hand, I tried to take in everything about her. Her eyes were large with long lashes—so like mine, only blue. Our hands were similar, and her way of speaking and mannerisms were all the same as mine. This was what I'd always wanted and more than I'd ever hoped for.

'Do you have any children?' I asked, trying to break the silence.

'Yes, four. Two girls and two boys. Linda, Robert, Stephanie and Christopher. The boys live with their father, my ex-husband,' she said as she looked at her hands in her lap.

As Farouk passed us our drinks, I made small talk to put her at ease. 'How long have you lived here?' I asked.

'Almost three years here, but I've lived around this area for almost ten.' She looked up at me then back at her hands.

'I left home when I was really young,' she began. 'Sixteen. I was going to be a nurse but somehow things turned out differently. A boy I knew asked me if I wanted to go to Darwin and on the spur of the moment, I said yes.'

She smiled as she said, 'It probably was the worst decision I've ever made but at the time it seemed right. I'd already signed up at a hospital for nurse training but I let it all go and I went to Darwin. I worked as a waitress up there for a while but eventually I hated it so much, I hitchhiked back.'

Wistfully she said, 'Sometimes I wish I could go back and do it right. I fell pregnant and had Linda before I married Tony, my first husband. After that, we had three kids of our own before things went bad and we got a divorce. Farouk was so good to me at that time. I really needed him and we've been together ever since.'

I could tell something was bothering her. She kept glancing up at me and opening her mouth as if to say something but then seemed to think better of it. Suddenly she looked up at me resolutely and said, 'Don't you remember me at all? My adoption papers said that I was almost four months old before I was adopted, and you were four years old.'

Years ago, I had tried to remember a baby but couldn't. Now there still just wasn't one in my memories.

I looked at her and shook my head. That wasn't the answer she wanted and she looked back down at her hands. I knew that for the rest of my life, I would never forget the look on her face as I told her that I had no memory of her. I knew she didn't understand why. I didn't know why myself.

'Tell me about your childhood, before you left home at sixteen,' I said, trying to change the subject.

Like a cloud crossing in front of the sun, a shadow passed over her face. I noticed a subtle change in her eyes, something indefinable as her face clouded and a small frown appeared between her eyebrows as if I'd trodden on forbidden land. I wondered what sadness had caused that reaction to my innocent question. It was an almost defensive attitude as if a barrier, firmly in place, had to be crossed in order to answer.

A small silence fell upon us before she continued haltingly.

'You know some of it,' she started. 'I was adopted when I was nearly four months old. My adoptive parents also adopted another girl who was older than me, called Jill. When I was four years old, our mother died.'

Her unhappiness was evident in every gesture.

'Unfortunately, probably because we were so young, Dad couldn't look after both of us. Jill was at school and I was still in preschool, so Dad decided that Jill would go and live with our grandmother and I would go to a home for girls for a few years till he got back on his feet again. I know he didn't want to do it but our grandmother could only take one of us. So he sent me to Nazareth House.'

CHAPTER 11

The Truth

I stared at her dumbfounded.

'Nazareth House? At Wynnum?'

'Yes, why?' she asked.

'I was there,' I whispered.

'You were at Nazareth?' Her eyes opened wide in surprise. 'When?'

'Well, let me see.' I had to stop and think of the dates. 'I went there when I was seven, so that would have been in 1962 and I left when I was twelve in 1967.'

'I went in when I was four, so that would have been 1963 and I left three years later in 1966,' she said.

The confused silence that followed slowly gave way to a growing understanding. I felt like I was in the twilight zone. The years and dates were racing through our minds and the dreadful realisation of what had happened started to dawn on us.

We had both been at Nazareth House at the same time!

We had actually spent countless weeks and months together, with no-one knowing we were sisters. She had been Sandra Stewart and I had been Patricia Gourgaud, and for three years we had lived with each other, eaten together and played together without even knowing who the other one was.

Had she been one of the little ones I dressed in the mornings or one of the ones I bathed at night? I wondered.

All of a sudden, I saw myself with Dad at Nazareth House in the concrete playground, sitting around a makeshift table drawing with me. Occasionally he would lean over to help another little girl whose parents hadn't visited. To think, he may have helped his other daughter Sandra without even knowing it.

I couldn't believe this.

'Do you remember Sister Philomena?' I asked, bewildered. I was finding it hard to accept the truth. I could see Sister Philomena with her hands hidden inside her sleeves standing in the corridor on my first night at Nazareth while I stood with my hands on my hips demanding to go home.

'Oh yeah,' she answered. 'Do you remember Mr Pinky?' She leant forward as she shot this question straight back at me.

'Oh, I remember Mr Pinky.' I was laughing and crying at the same time. A vision came to me of Sister Philomena standing over me with the shabby old pink hairbrush in her hand saying, 'For your sin of vanity, Patricia,' after I'd coloured in all my nails with a lead pencil.

'God, I remember dancing those Irish jigs in the playground. We had to keep our hands clenched and straight by our sides. Do you remember?' she asked quickly.

'Do I remember? God, how could I ever forget? To demonstrate the steps to us, she used to reach down and grab the hem of her skirt in each hand, holding her arms wide like Maria in *The Sound of Music* and showing black stockinged legs up to her knees. She used to hop from foot to foot and spin around so nimbly for someone of her size.'

I suddenly realised that I was smiling.

My expression sobered as I remembered lying awake terrified that first night listening for the sounds of claws on the wooden floors which meant the black dogs were looking for little girls' hands to eat. I could almost hear the sound of thunder and see the lightning flashes. I'd seen many movies over the years—*Damien, Omen II, The Exorcist* and many more—and in every single movie, bad things happened at night during a thunderstorm. I could almost see the huge tree outside the dormitory, lit up in outline every time there was a flash of lightning. It was so bare and skeletal, devoid of leaves and flowers in the winter months, that to an imaginative seven year old, alone and in a strange new place, it had seemed like it was reaching out to grab me.

'Did she ever tell you the story about the dogs coming in at night?' I asked. When I had been very little, I couldn't sleep until I'd checked under my bed at home at night for monsters. That stage quickly passed. Then I went to Nazareth.

'The ones that would eat you if you didn't keep your arms crossed over your chest every night?' she said. 'Boy, do I remember that. She scared the hell out of me.'

'And the concerts? The ones at Christmas?' I asked. Surely this couldn't be happening.

She nodded. 'Marilyn used to take me out by the poinciana tree. Do you remember that huge tree? She used to take me out by the tree and give me singing lessons when I joined the choir,' she continued. 'She was the one who needed the singing lessons.'

Both of us were leaning forward and talking quickly.

'You were in the choir, too?' I asked. There had only been about twelve girls in that choir. 'We were both in it?' This was incredible. We stared at each other. Our experiences were the same! Our memories were the same!

Memories of Marilyn jumped into my mind. I could almost hear her thin, quavery voice. She tried to give all of us singing lessons—the eldest girls, myself included, had totally ignored her but the younger ones weren't so lucky. I could still see her uneven crew-cut hair that had once been long and wavy. She had cried for days after the haircut, but the only comfort we could give her was that we all had the same style and we knew it would eventually grow back.

During my last year at Nazareth House, the choir had stood in St Bernard's Hall day after day singing 'Puff the Magic Dragon' while a nun faced us, her back to where the audience would be, silently mouthing the words and waving a baton in an attempt to keep our singing in time. I don't think any of us understood what she was trying to do.

A huge sadness came over me at the unfairness of it all. Neither of us would have been alone all those years—we would have had each other.

So many memories raced through my head. I felt like I was being drawn back into my past with the force of a whirlpool. I hadn't thought about those early years in such a long time. It hurt too much. I'd tried so hard to bury them deep in my sub-conscious. It wasn't that the years at the home were entirely bad. Sure, they had seemed that way to a little girl who had known freedom and then all of a sudden had it taken away. What had hurt more was that my whole life had been taken away from me along with a father who loved me and a mother who I desper-ately wanted to love me.

But it wasn't the orphanage that caused me the most pain. It was the dozens of foster homes I had visited over those years that had left scars. It had been all of those pious and 'holier than thou' hypocrites who had almost put me over the edge. The orphanage had been merely a stepping stone to those dreadful years. I think that in my mind, I'd reasoned that if I hadn't been at Nazareth House, I wouldn't have had to endure the bewilder-ing pain that those foster homes had caused me along with my feelings of insecurity and lack of self-worth. To myself I'd glori-fied those early lonely years in Spring Hill because the next stage in my life was so horrifying.

But I couldn't escape from my past. It would always be there.

Sometimes, in a strange way, I can almost be a little grateful to that past. Almost. It made me strong and very independent, the person I am today. I had been through so much and had come through it all; I knew that no matter what happened in the future I would be able to cope. Nothing would ever again take me to the depths of despair that I had once endured at the Andersons. Still, even though the outcome had left me a stronger, more self-reliant person, I silently wished God had thought about it a little longer and found another way to achieve this end. It was a hard lesson for a young girl to learn.

The one and only good thing that had happened while I stayed with the Andersons had been Mr Anderson mentioning a sister to me.

There was one thing I just couldn't fathom. Why didn't I remember a little baby at home with Mum and Dad? Even before that first visit to Nazareth House when I had been four years old, I just couldn't remember a baby at all.

Suddenly, I pulled myself up and said, 'Hang on. I was at Nazareth House twice; once when I was four years old and again when I was seven. That first time, I was only there for a few months before starting school in January 1960. I was born in 1955, when were you born?'

'September 22nd 1959,' she replied.

The difference was four years!

'That's why I don't remember a baby! I was at Nazareth House when you were born. By the time I came out, you must have already been adopted.'

Everything fell into place.

'Why did she give me up for adoption at four months old? They brought you back out of the home, why couldn't they keep us both?' She had a catch in her voice and I could tell this was going to be hard for both of us to understand. It looked like our mother had tried to keep her but something or someone had changed her mind. I had no answers for Sandra. No-one alive did.

A change had come over us both. This reunion was not a thing of gossamer dreams any more. Our own private memories had overshadowed our feelings of euphoria, leaving us confused and unhappy.

As I spoke, it was with a voice that sounded ill at ease.

'I guess I'd better go now.' I'd noticed it had turned midnight. 'I own a small coffee shop and I've got an early start in the morning. You probably do too. Can I call you tomorrow? Will you be home?'

'Yeah, I'll be home. Do you like working in the coffee shop?' she asked as she stood up.

'Nope,' I said instantly. 'But the kids and I have to eat.'

I said goodbye to Farouk and on the way to the front door, I turned and said, 'Are you sure it's all right to call you tomorrow?'

She nodded as she gave me a watery smile, the result of too many tears. It was just too much to take in on one night.

I could feel the knot of tension in my shoulders as I drove home and knew I would have trouble getting to sleep that night.

As the clock limped to 2 a.m., I stared with gritty eyes at the ceiling, replaying the words of the night over and over inside my head. My mind was like a kaleidoscope as I lay awake. Eventually I slept.

On many occasions over the years I've dreamt of my life at Nazareth House, but never have the dreams been as clear as the one I had that night.

I was standing at the gates to Nazareth, trying to enter but unable to because they were closed and padlocked. As I peered through the bars, no-one could be seen on the other side and briefly I wondered why I even wanted to be here at all. The driveway wound away from me and as I fought to see the huge building in the distance, darkness slowly began to fall. Twisted limbs from trees hung low over the unkempt driveway, nothing like I remembered.

I had a sense of evil things crouched low and menacingly in

the hidden recesses of the wildness waiting for me. My heart beat fast in my chest and tears came easily to my eyes.

Somehow, miraculously, I was through the gate.

The concrete was cracked and choked with weeds, and the tree roots protruded across the driveway like skeletal hands reaching for my ankles as I passed. Trees crowded together, their branches mingling to form an arch above my head, and the dank smell of wet soil came to me. Smaller trees grew between the larger ones, struggling to reach the diminishing sun. None of this was familiar to me.

Now and then, I caught sight of a flower, so pure and beautiful, hidden amongst the weeds and strangling shrubs. It receded into the dark ugliness that surrounded it, like the innocence of the children so many years ago, lost in the horror and pain, slowly becoming a part of the darkness themselves.

On and on I walked, sometimes thinking I was lost, pushing my way through the jungle growth. I hadn't thought the road was this long.

And then, there was Nazareth, silent and towering as I remembered it in the moonlight. Turning to my right, I could see in the distance the silvery moonlit water, so quiet and peaceful, not even a ripple to mar its beauty.

I turned back to the house and as I did, glanced towards the nuns' cemetery, now overgrown with weeds crawling across the graves on their way to take over the main house. In my dream, I floated across the weeds, being drawn inextricably towards lights that shone weakly in the windows.

As I stood silently in the empty hallway, I had a feeling that I wasn't alone. The house lived and breathed all around me. Doors stood ajar and I could hear the faint lilt of an Irish ballad playing softly in the distance amidst the whispering voices of young children.

A breath of wind came up and just as suddenly all lights were extinguished, leaving me terrified and alone in the darkness.

My fear, so long buried, was threatening my sanity and a scream was making its way up into my throat. Suddenly, I was awake, bathed in sweat with tears rolling down my face. To anyone watching, my eyes would have looked wild.

Eventually, the pounding of my heart slowed as the comfort of my room, thank God, fought its way through my terror.

CHAPTER 12

$\cdot\!\!\!+\!\!\!\cdot$

Groundhog Day

My alarm was set to go off at 5 a.m. but I was awake and up out of bed well before that.

As I opened my car door at 5.30 a.m., birds twittered their disapproval at me disturbing their morning rituals. *Oh, be quiet,* I thought. *I was up earlier than you.* The kookaburras started to laugh.

The sun was moving slowly up over the horizon and the trees were casting long shadows but this morning I had absolutely no urge to go to work. Especially to Wynnum where my coffee shop was situated.

It's funny how certain places keep drawing you back to them. Wynnum was my magnet. It seemed I always ended up back there. When I'd finally passed my Pizza Hut management exams, they'd sent me to Wynnum. When I was looking at coffee shops to buy, I'd finally bought one, again at Wynnum.

Every morning for the past three years, I'd done the same thing, five days a week, fifty-two weeks a year.

I left home and drove down Old Cleveland Road, turned left into Ricketts Road and then right into Greencamp Road. I drove past Tilley Road on my left, surprised that there were no roadworks holding up the traffic as they did every other morning. I then turned right into Manly Road until I reached Tingal Road.

Every morning as I crested the hill and started the final descent to the shop, Nazareth House loomed high on the horizon just a few miles ahead. Like a ghost haunting me. Every morning, my past was thrown back in my face. It was like having to live through a recurring nightmare . . . Groundhog Day! I'd often thought God might be a sadist. I'd tried for so long to tuck my past away in the dim recesses of my mind, but He kept on bringing it back into view, rubbing my nose in it, never letting me forget. Enforced therapy, you could call it.

Every morning as I looked out the front door of my shop, I could see the railway station. I'd stood in that same spot thirty odd years ago as a ten year old. To my left was Edith Street and I could just make out 'Crazy Clark's' where Woolworths had once stood.

Wynnum hadn't grown much since then. It still had only two main streets with little shops and offices facing each other. The barbershop was still there, and the jewellery stores. Replacing a few of the smaller clothing stores was a take-away chicken shop, a Chinese take-away and several little outdoor cafés. The shop owners were making an attempt at providing alfresco dining but the residents were still mainly elderly people and the effect was lost on them. It still surprised me that there had been virtually no changes over all the years. There was still no protection from the sun or rain and the benches on the footpaths were still always empty. The pensioners much preferred to sit in air-conditioned comfort out of the weather. With this in mind, I was attempting to lure them over to my shop. I had a good location, right near the railway station, and everyone had to pass my shop to go to the main shopping area. Unfortunately, that's exactly what they did some days—walk right past. But, like everyone else, I had good days and bad days.

This day, I opened my shop at 6.30 a.m. after putting pies,

roasts and a meatloaf in the big industrial gas oven. This morning, I did it without even thinking about what I was doing. I had too much on my mind.

The usual steady stream of customers coming from the trains came and went but my mind was not on my work. I filled the drink fridges, made a lasagne and a teacake as well as an apple shortcake and cut up the salads for sandwiches like a robot. My thoughts were with Sandra.

Margaret, my part-time helper, bustled in at 10 a.m. in time for the morning tea crowd, so I couldn't tell her what had happened until our break at 11 a.m., but she knew something had taken place. I couldn't stop smiling.

As I talked, I fiddled with the toasted cheese and tomato sandwich and cup of tea that would be my lunch. (On a good day, coffee was my breakfast.) I could barely form a coherent thought much less have a conversation with someone. 'What are the odds on something like this happening, Margaret?'

She looked at me over the top of her teacup and shrugged.

'I can't wait to see a photo of her. Does she look anything like you?'

'Yeah, I think so. When I first saw her, I thought, "I know you from somewhere." But you know what it was that was familiar? I could see myself in her face. She looks like me, particularly around the eyes and mouth. I only noticed just how much when I looked in the mirror this morning. You can definitely tell we're sisters. There's no doubt about that.'

As I talked, a warm feeling ran through me, a sense of belonging at last. I'd never had a feeling that was so strong before. I wanted so much to be a part of my sister's life, it hurt.

I jumped up and said, 'I'm going to call her.'

'What are you going to say?' Margaret asked.

'I don't know. Just hello.'

I rang Sandra's number and when she answered, I felt a familiar lump in my throat.

'Hi,' I said. 'I just wanted to say hello. I don't have much to say. I really just wanted to hear your voice again.' I was beginning to feel foolish.

'I was just thinking about you,' she said almost shyly. 'I rang Paula this morning and she wants us to go and see her on Saturday. Are you doing anything?'

'Not a thing,' I said. It didn't matter if I was. I would have changed my plans anyway. I wanted to see Sandra again.

'I was thinking last night after you went home. I'm going to write back to Children's Services and get what they call Unidentifying Information,' she said. 'That's supposed to give you more information about your adoption and parents that's not included in the first lot of papers. Maybe it will tell us some things about what happened. I really need to know. I keep looking at my birth certificate. Open, close, open, close, to see if it's really true. I can't help feeling that it's just not fair. All these years wasted, you know?'

'I know what you mean. I feel the same way.'

I could hear voices filtering into the shop and I knew Margaret would have her hands full soon so, as much as I hated to, I had to go.

'Look, I'm sorry, I'm not brushing you off or being rude, but I have to go. It's starting to get busy here, so I'll ring you later, okay?'

'You don't have to do that. I'm all right. Really I am. If you like, just meet me at my house tomorrow at about 10 a.m. and we'll go to Paula's together. She doesn't live too far from here. Is that fine by you?'

'Sure. I'm really looking forward to it.' I could hear more customers coming into the shop. 'I've really got to go but I'll see you tomorrow at ten. Okay? Bye.'

'Bye,' she almost whispered, and hung up.

CHAPTER 13

---+---

Out of the Shadows

My thoughts about our meeting with Paula at this time, I'm ashamed to say, were partly selfish. I looked forward to meeting her, but I had an ulterior motive. I was desperate for any information about my father, no matter how inconsequential it may have seemed; I wanted it all. I needed to know everything about him.

When had Paula last seen him? Did she have photos? How had he died? Where was he buried?

I dug desperately through my memories but just couldn't picture him. *How could I forget something so important? His face, for goodness sake!*

My thoughts drifted back and I remembered occasions we'd spent together as if they were yesterday, but it was as though his face was in the shadows just out of reach, out of focus.

I remembered the time walking hand in hand with Dad down the hill to busy Wickham Terrace when the Queen visited. He perched me on top of his shoulders to catch a glimpse of 'Her Majesty' waving as her car drove past us. I remembered how my father had led me by the hand on Anzac Day as we marched proudly in the parade with the men of the 9th Division on our way to Anzac Square.

I remembered the hat he always wore, and the gentle smiles and tender hugs. I could even feel his touch and his goodnight kiss.

I just couldn't *see* him.

Saturday was a typical beautiful March day with clear blue skies and a few clouds that looked like they'd been shot out of a whipped cream can.

I picked up Sandra and Farouk at their house and as we drove to Paula's, the car was filled with a heavy silence, with none of us knowing what we might be walking into. Neither Sandra nor I had anticipated the nerves we both felt as we approached the house.

Paula was now a woman of fifty, thirteen years older than Sandra and nine years older than me, but still I felt very tentative about meeting her. In her shoes, I'm not sure how I would have reacted. She was, after all, meeting two children from the relationship of her father and his mistress: the same woman who took her father away from her mother when she was nine. The best we could hope for was that she didn't treat us with animosity.

As we passed through the front gate, we could hear a buzzer going off inside the house, obviously letting Paula know that we had arrived. The path to her house ran alongside a forest of a garden that let in sparse light to the ferns massed around the trees. Before we could knock, Paula was standing at the door.

She was taller than both of us, slim, with hair as dark as Dad's had been. Her large eyes with long dark lashes were the same size as ours but they were a soft blue, much the same as Sandra's. She had an air of self-confidence as she greeted us with a smile.

We needn't have worried how she would react to us; she was obviously pleased to see Sandra and me.

After she gave us all a hug and introductions were quickly made, she said, 'Come on in,' and we trooped single file through her lounge room to a cosy kitchen where a middle-aged man stood beside a table that was laden with enough food for an army. She said, 'This is Barry, my husband.'

I looked at Barry, trying to recognise the man I had met at the Exhibition. I barely remembered his face from so many years ago, so I had no chance of recognising him now. He was in his early fifties with a full head of grey hair and a quick smile.

'Please sit down,' he said.

Paula looked at me, smiled and said, 'Promise me you won't throw up on my carpet.'

'Excuse me?' I was totally confused and a little insulted. What on earth did she mean by that?

'Did Sandra tell you that I remembered you from when we went to the Exhibition?' she asked with a smile on her face.

'Yes, she did,' I replied, still not knowing where this conversation was going.

'Don't you remember what happened when we left? The taxi? Surely you couldn't forget that.'

'Oh, God. I do!' Suddenly it all came back to me. 'The taxi. I threw up in the back of it. Now I remember!' I could feel myself blushing as the end of that day came back to me. 'After all that rubbish I ate, I went on a ride in sideshow alley. The Beatle Bug, wasn't it?'

'That's right. I can still see the look on the taxi driver's face when he glanced over his shoulder at his new décor in the back seat. What a spectacular colour it was. I doubt that the extra money Dad gave him made up for the time spent cleaning and airing his cab for the rest of the night.'

I was feeling very embarrassed as I said, 'I hope I make a

better impression this time. I had no idea who you were, or that you were my sister.'

She was nodding as I spoke, and finally said, 'Yep, that was me. You stayed with Barry and me for that weekend.'

'God, you were a quiet kid,' he said. 'You hardly said a word the whole time.'

'I must admit,' Paula continued with a half-smile, 'I was very dubious about this meeting. Mr Anderson rang me looking for you when you ran away all those years ago. After he told me you had gone wild, I had visions of someone with tattoos and multiple body-piercings turning up on my doorstep in leather after stepping off a bike.'

Unwanted thoughts of that bastard jumped into my mind. All the sleepless nights I'd spent listening for the creaks outside my door. The many nights sitting on his lap while his hands ran up and down my legs as I gritted my teeth and tried to think of anything but what was happening. I remembered sitting in the corner of my room feeling sick to my stomach and sobbing quietly, praying God would take me and put me anywhere else but where I was. I'm sure Mr Anderson didn't tell Paula all the hideous things he'd made me endure over those three years, and I could barely keep the bitterness from my voice as I said, 'Don't believe everything you hear, Paula.'

As we sat and drank cup after cup of coffee, reminiscing came easily.

'You know,' she said, 'you probably have as many memories of Dad as I do.'

She said it with a little barb in her voice. Not really aimed at me, but aimed at circumstances as they were. I realised then that I wasn't the only one who adored and missed him. The hurt had not stopped with me—Paula and her family had been affected as well. It hadn't occurred to me before. I'd been so engrossed in how I felt, I hadn't looked past my own feelings.

'When he left us, he only came back every now and then to see us, sometimes with Pop. You remember Pop, don't you?'

I nodded. I remembered the white-haired magician who produced coins from behind my ears.

'He adored kids,' Paula said.

Then 'Do you remember they both loved horseracing?' she mused. 'One Saturday, Dad and Pop had been to the races, and as I stood in the front yard expecting them at any moment, I saw them both coming down the road—on opposite sides of the street. Neither of them were talking or looking at each other and the expressions on their faces were as black as thunder. It looked so funny, but it was obvious that they'd lost their money.'

She stood up abruptly, walked into the lounge room and came back with some photos, handing them to Sandra and me with a smile.

And there he was! Finally out of the shadows, and back in focus, DAD.

Tears rolled down my face and I openly cried as I saw him smiling back at me, so handsome and familiar, as though he was pleased to see me again after all these years. It was a black and white photo taken when he was in Egypt during World War II, standing in his uniform, hands behind his back and legs slightly apart. I wanted to hold that photo close to my heart and pretend it was Dad I was holding.

Through all of this, Sandra sat and listened silently, not able to participate, not knowing anything about this man we were discussing. Fragmented as our memories were, she had nothing like we had, no memories at all. All she had was this black and white photo of a stranger, and Paula, yet another stranger, telling her that this man was her father.

It didn't occur to me at the time that the coming years of adjustment would be hard for us all as we learnt about each other, becoming not only friends but sisters as well. I was totally oblivious to all this then. All I knew was that I was happy. I now had my sister, plus a half-sister, photos and loads of memories.

'I would have taken you, you know,' Paula said as she looked down at her hands. She lifted her head and said, 'But I had kids of my own by then. A two year old and a set of twins. I just couldn't.'

'Oh, Paula, I don't feel bad about all that. Don't even think that.' I was sad to see her distressed.

On my way home, I decided the afternoon had turned out better than I could have expected. The trepidation at meeting Paula was long forgotten and I had the bonus of a copy of Dad's death certificate in my hand.

I walked into the house, put my bag down on the bench and sat down in the lounge room after turning on the television. I needed some mindless entertainment to rest my brain. I tried to pay attention to the soapie that was on, but I finally just closed my eyes and rested my head back.

What would have happened if Paula had taken me out of the home? I wouldn't be here now, I thought. I wouldn't have met my ex-husband and I wouldn't have had my two boys. I probably wouldn't have worked at Greenslopes Hospital, which meant I wouldn't have met David.

He and I had kept in touch after he'd married and left Greenslopes Hospital to join the air force. Over the years, he and his wife had moved around wherever the air force had sent them and had two boys whose ages were in between those of my two boys. They'd finally settled in Melbourne when David left the armed forces and joined a commercial airline. That had been six years ago.

His wife had been pretty sick of moving around by then and had given him an ultimatum. Leave the air force or I leave you. So, he left the air force. But things never seemed to pick up between them after that and a year later they divorced.

Time and tide had flowed around David and me for many years with neither of us having the opportunity to express any hidden feelings for each other. Recently, chance or fate had brought us together.

I never thought I'd fall in love with my best friend. Someone who had known me when I was young and could touch my face, and trace the lines around my eyes with love and familiarity.

My daydream was interrupted by the sound of the front door screen banging shut as Tony came bounding in with Oscar thrown over his shoulder, patting him on the back like he was burping a baby.

'Mum, can I have two dollars to go up to the PCYC?' With Tony, more so than Mark, every waking moment at the weekends was spent playing basketball.

'Sure. Just get it out of Emily.' Emily was my money pig. All my spare change went into Emily for any little expenses. He rummaged around in it with Oscar's paws jiggling over his shoulder. As he scraped a handful of money into his pocket, I exclaimed, 'Hey, don't take all of Emily's money!'

He looked at me as if I was demented.

'Emily's money? It's a pottery pig, Mum.'

'Yeah, well. Don't take it all.'

He sped out of the room, yelled out, 'I'm going to Lee's. See ya,' and was gone.

Life goes on, I thought.

I stood up and went into the kitchen to make a cup of coffee, and glanced over at Dad's death certificate, which I had placed on the bench when I walked in. I'd almost forgotten about it. While the kettle boiled, I sat down in the armchair by the window and looked at it.

Cause of death—emphysema of lungs, coronary artery occlusion, and pulmonary tuberculosis.

Maiden name of mother—Beatrice Matilda Nairn.

Died—July 25th 1968. Buried at Nudgee Cemetery.

Issue living—Paula 22, Terrance John 20, Sharon Therese 16.

Something was niggling at me but I didn't know what.

The cause of death was as I would have expected and I

already knew of the other two children in Paula's family. What was bothering me?

And then it hit me. The date!

July 25th 1968!

I ran to get a pen to work out the maths, so that I could be sure.

There was no mistake.

I had been thirteen years old in 1968. July was in the middle of winter and the beginning of the second semester in high school.

Flashes of sitting for those hours in the waiting room of the Children's Department came to me and the tears on the way home with Mr Anderson telling me my father had been drunk.

I was filled with anger and confusion at Mr Anderson's terrible deception. How could anybody be so cruel? Dad hadn't been drunk at all! He had died!

All those years of pain and of misjudging my father need never have been! All those years of wondering why he'd deserted me and left me to my fate could have been avoided. The anger and hate resurfaced again at the thought of those years in the care of Mr Anderson. As if he hadn't hurt me enough! What sick satisfaction could a grown man get from demoralising a child? *I hope you rot in hell*, I thought.

I cried, feeling like I had done nothing else for the past two weeks. I'd thought I'd finally put this part of my life behind me, especially after having found my sister, and now, here it was, all over again only worse. It was like tearing a scab off a nearly healed wound and leaving it open and bleeding again. I'd come to terms with my childhood, rationalising that out of everything bad comes something good—but nothing had prepared me for this new sorrow.

CHAPTER 14

✦

But Wait . . . There's More

Sandra and I started to settle into our new roles. The very next weekend, she came over for afternoon tea. We were still a little nervous, each of us trying to please the other one, on our best behaviour.

While I made the coffee, she walked outside to sit at the table and chairs under the pergola. I loved this area with all its hanging plants and ferns everywhere. I called it 'my jungle'.

My dog, a lovable Doberman by the name of Zoe, came bounding over to Sandra, waiting patiently for the pat she hoped was coming. Zoe was a legacy of David's. He had moved in with me several months ago and had brought her with him. She was wonderful company for me when he was away and both my boys were doing their own thing.

'How can you stand to have a black dog?' Sandra asked.

I knew exactly what she meant. It had taken me many years to overcome my phobia about black dogs. 'I couldn't for years,' I said, 'but as I grew older I realised just how stupid I was being. Sister Philomena's story about the black dogs couldn't possibly be true. It was just a story to keep all the children in their beds at night.'

I could see her staring at Zoe.

'Do you remember the long walks the nuns used to take us on?' She looked at me. 'We used to walk hand in hand down to the front gate and back again through the paddocks. Saturdays after hair washing, I think it was.'

I nodded, remembering well the cowpats that we had to avoid.

'I remember one Saturday when Sister Philomena took us for a walk. We had almost reached the gate when we all saw a large black dog on the outside of the gate, sitting and watching us while saliva dripped off its tongue. We all stopped and gasped as we turned to look at Sister Philomena. I remember being so scared.'

Sandra was looking down at her hands again. She had a habit of doing that when she was thinking about things that were painful for her. She looked up at me and continued.

'She said to all of us, "Children, make a sign of the cross and say, 'Jesus, Mary and Joseph, protect me'." Everyone remembered vividly the stories of devils and black dogs so we hurriedly crossed ourselves. When we turned back to look at the gate, the dog had gone!' She laughed. 'I suppose the sight of fifty noisy children bearing down on you is enough to make any sane person, let alone a dog, turn tail and run. At the time, that never occurred to any of us. We thought this was the best magic we had ever seen and we all walked back quickly, thanking Jesus, Mary and Joseph for protecting us and knowing that our hands would definitely be staying in bed that night.'

I sat there staring at her with my mouth agape. Sometimes I felt the world tilting crazily. I remembered that happening. I'd been there at the gate, too.

I looked at her and again saw the resemblance between us. How could the nuns at Nazareth not have seen it as well? We didn't remember each other but we had been children. Surely the obvious resemblance that existed between us now was obvious then. I wished to God that it had been noticed.

The hours passed by quickly and soon she rose to leave.

'Why don't you ring Farouk and see if he wants to come over for dinner?' I asked. I didn't want to let her go.

'Depends on what's for dinner,' she said playfully.

I grinned as I said, 'Your choice. Tripe or haddock?'

'Oh, God. You just lost me. Never again in my life will I eat tripe or haddock. I can't even stand the smell of either of them. Three years of eating that stuff in the home is enough to last me a lifetime. No, I'm going home for a pizza.'

Two weeks later, Sandra rang while I was standing in the shower. She did this so often, it seemed as if she knew when to ring.

I grabbed the towel from the rack and threw it on the carpet before standing on it to answer the bedroom phone.

'Hello,' I said breathlessly.

'It's me,' she said simply. 'Can you come and see me? I've received my bits in the mail and you're just not going to believe what it says.'

'Can't you tell me over the phone? You've done it again. I'm in the shower,' I laughingly replied.

'Oh, no. You've got to see this to believe it.' She was serious.

'Okay. I'll probably be an hour by the time I get dressed. Is that all right?' I asked. My curiosity was getting the better of me.

'Sure,' she said. 'See you soon.'

The letter from the State Children's Department read:

At the time of adoption it was not departmental practice to obtain detailed background information from birth parents as is the case today. As such, there is no record of any physical descriptions, special interests, hereditary traits or medical information.

It appears that at the time of your birth on September 22nd, 1959, your birth mother was living as 'man and wife' with your birth father. It was her intention to care for you herself and she said that your birth father was willing to support you both. Your birth mother signed a consent for your adoption in January 1960. No reason is recorded for her change of intention.

Your birth mother had two daughters born 1952 and 1955 who were also adopted. Your sister born on 16th March 1952 is named Annette Maud Miner and your sister born on 21st May 1955 was named Patricia Therese Gourgaud.

Neither of us could believe the comments at the bottom of the letter.

Another sister?

'Let's ring Paula. She may know something. What do you think?' I said, still in a daze. Sandra was just sitting with her hands on the table, holding the letter but not saying a word.

'Sandra? What do you think?' I repeated.

'Huh? Oh—I guess so. I don't know what to think any more.'

I plugged in the kettle, reached for two mugs and put a tea bag and two teaspoons of sugar in each one before digging around in my bag for my address book. I turned to the 'G' section for Paula's number. Even though she was now married and had a different surname, she was still very proud of her maiden name and we had a standing joke between us, calling each other 'Ms P. Gourgaud'.

Paula answered the phone after only a couple of rings.

'Hi, Paula. It's Trish here. Have you got a couple of minutes to spare?'

'Sure,' she said. 'What's up?'

I glanced over at Sandra. She was still sitting at the table looking at the letter. 'Sandra received her papers in the mail today and you'll never guess in a million years what they say.'

'What?'

'They say that we have another sister, four years older than me, who was adopted at birth. I thought you might know something about this. My first thought was to call you.'

After a slight hesitation, she said, 'Was she one of the twins?'

'Twins?' I asked, dumbfounded. 'What twins?'

Sandra's head snapped up and her mouth opened in amazement.

For goodness sake, what next? I thought. I felt like Alice in Wonderland, falling down a hole and finding myself in another place where everything was different and weird. I'd studied chemistry at school, but I hadn't learnt too much, apart from discovering that you could throw something extra into a test tube and it could blow up with a bang. We'd just found that something extra. That's how I felt.

'I'm not sure of the details,' Paula started, 'but I remember Dad coming home to visit us one day saying that there had been a set of twins. I haven't any idea what age I was.'

This was getting out of control.

'Paula, are you sure he said that? There wasn't any mention of twins in Sandra's letter. Do you think you could have been mistaken? God, how many kids did they have?' I asked.

The kettle was boiling softly, so I turned it off and started pouring water into each of the mugs. Still balancing the phone, I opened the fridge and found the milk. I glanced at Sandra to see if she minded me rummaging around in her kitchen. Although sisters, we were still strangers to each other in many ways, and a woman's kitchen is her own private domain. She hadn't even looked up from the letter.

'I suppose I could be mistaken,' Paula said hesitantly, 'but I can almost hear his words. Maybe he was talking about someone else. I just don't know. I was very young.' She had sounded so sure to start with, but was gradually getting more doubtful as she continued. 'I wish I could help, but I don't really know anything.'

As I put milk into each cup and then returned it to the fridge, I said, 'You know what I'm going to do? I'm going to request my papers as well from Children's Services. I'd like to get my own original birth certificate anyway, and maybe there'll be something in my papers that isn't in Sandra's.'

'Sure,' she said. 'Can't hurt.'

I hung up and walked over to Sandra with her cup in my hand. 'Here. Drink this,' I said. It sounded like an order.

She sipped the tea and made a face. 'Sweet,' was all she said.

'It'll do you good.' My voice was low, barely a whisper. 'Everyone knows that sweet tea is the remedy for any shock. You're half Irish so you must know that. It's bred into us.'

I knew she was having a hard time with everything. I, at least, had had some hint that she existed. This was all so overwhelming for her. As she had once said to me, she had only started all of this to find a mother. So, I didn't come up with any solutions or theories. I was just there. I didn't want to talk at all. I just wanted to wait for her lead.

CHAPTER 15

⟊

Butterflies in my Stomach

First thing on Monday morning, I rang Children's Services and asked them to fax me the appropriate forms. I filled them out and by the end of the week, I posted them back. In the meantime, while I waited for the papers to arrive, we had a sister to find.

'Okay,' I said to Sandra, 'let's start in the phone book again. That's where you started when you were looking for me.' It was now the following Saturday and I'd spent the entire week wishing for it to end. 'She'll probably be married but we may be lucky and find a brother or parents or some relative. Where's your phone book?'

Sandra went over to the phone table and brought back the White Pages opened at the 'M's.

'There are over two full columns of Miners. This'll take all night,' she said.

'Well, I guess we can start tonight and see how far we get. Tomorrow, we split the rest and you ring half and I'll ring the other half. All right?'

'Okay,' she said. 'You start first.'

It took only three calls before an elderly sounding Mrs Miner said, 'Yes, I have a daughter called Annette.'

She listened quietly as I innocently, and perhaps naively, told her my story of a newly found sister and how I hoped I'd traced Annette to this number.

Afterwards there was a long silence. I almost thought the connection had been broken then I heard her take a breath and speak. 'I've been dreading this day all of Annette's life. My husband and I adopted Annette at birth as well as a boy seven years before her. Neither of them knows they're adopted. And I'm not going to tell them,' she said to me with growing agitation. 'I'll lose her. She won't love me any more and I can't risk that. Does your mother want to meet her, too?'

'Our mother is dead, Mrs Miner,' I told her. 'It's just Sandra and me, now.'

'Oh,' was all she said. I thought she sounded a little relieved.

Her pain touched me as I tried desperately to reassure her.

'We're not taking her away from you, Mrs Miner. We just want to share her,' I said. I had an overwhelming urge to make her understand. 'No-one can take Annette away from you. You will always be her mother. You were the one who tucked Annette into bed when she was little. It was you who bandaged the scraped knees and who was there on the first day of school, graduation and marriage. It's not just having a baby that creates a bond; it's the day-to-day living and caring that makes a relationship. You're more her mother than the woman who gave birth to Annette. It's only a myth that the act of giving birth immediately makes you maternal or gives you the ability to be a mother. She will always love you. You are her mother.'

Still, no matter what I said, she would not change her mind. She flatly refused to give me Annette's married name or her phone number.

We ended our fairly heated conversation with my vow to

her, 'I'm not giving up, you know. No matter what you say, I'm not giving up.'

I was angry at what I saw as selfishness in the woman.

'You've had her to yourself all of her life.' I knew I sounded desperate but I couldn't help it. 'Sandra and I have spent our whole lives not knowing her, and now it's our turn.'

'You'll end up killing my husband,' she said as she started to cry. 'He's not well. This will be on your head. This will kill him.'

'I'm sorry for all of this. I really am. But you have to see it from our side as well. It's not fair what you're asking me to do. Surely you see that, don't you?'

'Please don't do this,' she begged.

'I have to. The best I can do is to call you when I find her married name and address. I will keep looking, you know. But I promise I'll think seriously about what you've said before I do anything. That's the best I can offer.'

'Thank you,' she said before she hung up.

In hindsight, this pretty speech was probably just as selfish of me. I was possibly too eager to get on with this next phase of my life and it hadn't occurred to me yet that maybe some things are best left alone.

But I was unstoppable and unrelenting. I had been given a challenge and was oblivious to the possible distress that the outcome could cause, only knowing that I had been deprived of my family for forty-one years and the fighting Irish in me was not about to give up and stop looking now. The possibility of failure never entered my mind.

Sandra had listened to every word.

'What do we do?' she asked.

'We keep looking,' was all I said.

Mrs Miner had unwittingly given us the key to finding Annette by telling us she also had an adopted son. With renewed determination, Sandra and I went back to the phone book once more, looking for Annette's brother, knowing this would be easier since his name would still be Miner.

Again, after only a few calls, a woman answered the phone and said, 'Yes, I know Annette Miner. She's my sister-in-law but she's not Miner any more. She's married. Her name is Sullivan now. Who did you say was speaking?'

I looked at Sandra and put my index finger and thumb together in the universal gesture of 'okay' as I continued. Having been bitten once, I knew I would have to change my story. This time, I made no mistake.

'I'm an old school friend and I'm organising a school reunion. Do you think you could give me her phone number and address so we can contact her?' I crossed my fingers.

'Sure. But I doubt if she would be able to come. She lives in Cairns now and has done since her husband died. She remarried and went to live there about thirteen years ago.' I could hear papers rustling. 'Here it is,' she said. 'Do you have a pen?'

I wrote the number down and thanked her, marvelling at the ease with which this white lie had succeeded. I hung up feeling very pleased with myself, although a little guilty at the deception.

'You call her,' Sandra said.

'Not right now; let's think about it. You heard what Mrs Miner said. Annette doesn't even know she's adopted. Do we have the right to do this? You know, she may not even be the right Annette Miner. Stranger things have happened. Have you thought about that?' My conscience was telling me to stop. 'I even promised Mrs Miner that I would ring her first,' I continued, stalling.

'We'll ring her from the airport,' Sandra said determinedly.

'No, Sandra. Come on, let's think it over tonight.'

'One night,' Sandra said, holding up a finger.

136

That night, I lay awake for hours thinking about whether what we were doing was right. My mind was running in circles and I could feel a headache coming on behind my eyes. A tension headache.

A lot depended on this decision; people's lives would change because of it. But if we didn't call Annette, we would forever wonder if that had been the right decision. Didn't she have a right to know the truth? Mrs Miner had been wrong not to tell her about the adoption. She should have been the one to tell her, not me, I thought. If Annette had decided not to contact her birth family, that would have been Annette's decision. But instead, she had never been given that choice. I knew it had been done out of love but it had still been wrong. It was Annette's right to know the truth.

It may not even be her, I thought. The clincher would be the birth date given in the letter from Children's Services. If it matched with hers, then we had the right person.

So with butterflies in my stomach, I made the call the next morning.

She answered the phone with a bright 'Hello.'

'Annette Sullivan?' I asked.

'Yes,' she replied.

'I'm sorry to bother you,' I haltingly started, 'but could you tell me if your maiden name was Annette Miner?'

'Yes, it was,' she answered with a slight question in her voice.

'Annette Maud Miner?'

'Yes.'

'And is your birth date the sixteenth of March 1952?'

'Yes, it is,' she said. 'Why are you asking?' I could hear her wariness growing.

We'd actually found her. But again, not having thought first about what I was going to say, I'd walked into a situation like I was John Wayne, with all my guns blazing,

'I'm sorry,' I started, 'I can't tell you right now but I promise I'll ring you back tonight.'

'Did somebody die?' she quickly asked.

'No, no, nothing like that,' I replied, as reassuringly as I could. 'I really am sorry, but I'll explain it all tonight,' and hung up.

Now if someone had left me high and dry like that, I would have gone mental, but I felt I had no other choice. I needed to think this through. I was again starting to have doubts about what we were doing.

Annette was forty-four now and so many people's lives could be affected by this next call to her. Did I have the right to make it? On the other hand, I was ecstatic at having not one sister, but two! All my thoughts from the night before ran through my head again, but my doubts were quickly overridden by the prospect of future happiness and I could hardly contain myself. I knew that, deep down, I desperately wanted to make that call; the lure of my elusive family was too much for me to ignore.

That night after telling Sandra what I was going to do, I rang Annette. She answered after only one ring, obviously waiting for the call.

I took a deep breath and launched into the story.

'I'm sorry about this morning, but I had some things to think over.' I was so nervous my hands were shaking as I held the phone. 'My name is Patricia and I was adopted when I was quite young. About six weeks ago, I had a phone call from a woman by the name of Sandra who has also been adopted and who has recently discovered that she has a sister. Through a long process, she discovered the sister was me. She sent away for more information from Children's Services and they sent a letter back saying that we also had an older sister. They gave us the name and birth date.'

'What has this got to do with me?' she asked.

'You're our older sister,' I stated bluntly.

There was complete silence at the other end of the phone. Then, 'But that can't be true,' she said. 'I already have a mother and father.'

'Yes, I know,' I haltingly started. 'I spoke to Mrs Miner yesterday and told her the story, and she eventually admitted to me that you and your brother were both adopted. She said she didn't tell you then and won't tell you now because she's scared of losing you.'

'I . . . I . . . I can't believe it. How is Mum? Is she upset you called me?'

'I haven't told her yet. I wanted to talk to you about that.'

'There has to be some other explanation. I just can't believe this. This is all too much for me to take in.' She was denying everything. What else had I expected? 'I've got to think about all this. Does Paul know, too?'

'If Paul is your brother, then no, I haven't told him anything. That's up to you if you want to tell him.'

'I've got to find out for myself if this is true. I can't think right now. I'll have to call you back after I sort this out.'

I gave her my number and sat back, praying I'd done the right thing.

I don't know what I expected but this wasn't it. I felt empty. Had I expected her to open her arms to me straight away? It had been very unrealistic of me to think that would happen. Of course she would be upset. How stupid of me to think that she wouldn't be. I tried to put myself in her shoes but I couldn't. I'd never had a normal family life and I couldn't imagine what it would feel like. *Oh, God, I hope I've done the right thing.*

As promised, she called a few days later with endless questions.

'I've written to Children's Services and requested my own papers,' she said determinedly. 'I have to see it for myself in black and white. In the meantime, could you ring my mother back and tell her that you decided not to contact me? Both my parents are in their seventies now and I don't want anything to upset them.

Besides, Dad's not well. If it turns out that we are sisters, I probably won't tell them anyway. I'd rather their last few years were happy ones.'

With this sentiment in mind, I was able to make that call to Mrs Miner.

CHAPTER 16

✦

For She Means the World . . .

The ensuing weeks of occasional phone calls between Annette and Sandra and me brought an acceptance by her that we probably were her sisters, and during this time, we learnt about each other's backgrounds.

'I'd always lived in Brisbane,' she started, 'until about twenty years ago when my husband and I moved to Townsville. Allan was my second husband. I married way too young the first time and got a divorce a couple of years later.'

I could hear her take a deep breath before she continued. 'Allan and I had three children before we moved up there. We bought a house and were trying to do it up ourselves. One day, he was standing on a stool fixing a light fitting and something went wrong. All he could say was, "Turn the electricity off, Annette." By the time I got back inside the house, he was dead. He'd been electrocuted. I felt so empty for ages. I couldn't even cry for a while. Shock, I guess.'

'Do you want to talk about this? You don't have to, you know,' I said, hearing the sorrow in her voice.

'No, it's fine. That was thirteen years ago. You never really get over something like that but you have to keep going. After all, I had three little girls to look after. Anyway, Don was a close friend of ours and he helped me when he could. After a while, we fell in love and moved to Cairns, and Mary came along.'

'You've got four girls?' I asked.

'Yes. Mary is the last one.'

'You're very lucky,' I said. 'I would have given my eyeeteeth to have a girl.'

'It's not all fun and games. Four girls are a lot of work.' There was silence for a few seconds before she said, 'I've been thinking. Last week, you spoke about a man you thought was Mum's brother. Uncle Terry, was it?' She was hungry for any information I could give her—absolutely anything—and she had homed in on one of my age four memories. 'Where is he?'

I hadn't even thought of contacting him, but she was right!

As a four year old, I remembered visiting a man Dad had called 'Uncle Terry'. I was sure that this was Mum's brother.

I grabbed the phone book and found to my amazement a Terrence Mooney living only twenty minutes from me and only ten minutes from Sandra.

'You know, there's a Terrence Mooney in the phone book living at Waterford. Surely, it can't be this easy to find him?' I said, shaking my head.

'Why not?' she said. 'You found me quite easily.'

All these years, I thought, *and he was right here!*

I could hear the enthusiasm in Annette's voice. 'I know he won't know me, but I want to call him. Do you mind?'

'No, I guess not.' I wasn't sure if that was the best way to go about it but she sounded definite. 'If you're sure you want to.'

'Yes, I am. Sandra called you and you called me. Now it's my turn to call Uncle Terry.'

'Okay,' I said dubiously. 'Ring me back after you've spoken to him. And don't forget it's an STD phone call. It'll cost you a fortune,' I reminded her.

'I'll call tonight. The rates are cheaper after seven. I'll ring you back tomorrow and let you know what happens—wish me luck!'

The next day, Annette rang to say that she had talked to Uncle Terry for almost an hour, while she gave him a sketchy rendition of the past few weeks.

To my amazement, Annette said he remembered me instantly. As expected, he didn't remember anything about Annette and I could hear the disappointment in her voice. As much as she would have liked to know more details, he was unable to remember any. He hadn't been able to tell her much at all.

Now it was Sandra's and my turn to meet him, although Sandra was very nervous and unsure of what to expect. I had already rung Uncle Terry to introduce myself and we arrived at his house at the prearranged time, me all smiles and Sandra quiet as a church mouse.

I had the feeling that everything was taking its toll on her and she felt out of her depth. She had started all this by trying to find her parents and it was all snowballing for her. But I loved this role of 'big sister'. I had wanted it for as long as I could remember. I also knew that meeting Uncle Terry must have seemed for her like meeting a ghost connected to another ghost.

We pulled up outside a low brick house with a tidy garden and a trellis of flowers covering a walkway to the front door. I gave Sandra a reassuring hug as I told her, 'Everything will be fine. Trust me. How many times have I lied to you in your life?'

She gave me a 'you've got to be kidding' look and said with a smirk, 'Ha ha! Very funny!'

A once tall, but now slightly stooped, and wiry elderly man greeted us at the door. I had no recollection of this grey-haired man with his strong square jaw and pale, watery hazel eyes, and because he hadn't seen me since I was four years old, he wouldn't have recognised me either. But he still smiled at me as I hugged him. He gestured us in like a friendly old butler, ushering us into a room that was small but well kept and loved. It was like I'd stepped into a picture gallery. There were photos of children everywhere; over the walls, on a side table, on a bureau. Everywhere.

'They're here,' Uncle Terry called out.

A tiny, frail old woman came out from the kitchen. When she smiled at us, it was like the sun coming out from behind clouds. She was so thin and fragile, and hugging her was like hugging a bundle of sticks, but she smelt like a flower—lavender. Following her were two women and a man.

'This is my wife, Laurel, and these are three of our children, Donna, Roslyn and Brian.'

I recognised them from some of the pictures on the walls. We hadn't expected to see anyone else and I could feel Sandra's tension. Brian had black hair and looked so much like his father that I could imagine that was how Uncle Terry had looked when he was young. You could tell that both women were sisters although Roslyn had dark hair and Donna had long fair hair that fell in waves down her back. As I looked around at the photos on the wall, I saw where my fair hair had come from. So many times I'd looked in the mirror and wondered about it. Four of the seven children had fair hair. I truly did belong in this family.

'Can I make you a cup of tea?' Aunt Laurel asked us in a low, breathy voice.

'That would be wonderful. Thank you,' I said.

Uncle Terry told us to sit down as he started to tell us about himself. He was now seventy-five. He had been the elder of two brothers my mother had had, and together with Laurel had raised seven children right here in Brisbane. He had lost contact with his sister many years ago, after I went to Nazareth House; the last he heard of her had been when a man she had been living with rang to say that Merle had died.

'I don't remember a baby being born before you,' he said to me. 'I do know Merle had a baby when you were just a little tyke, Patricia. I think the baby was about three months old when she came home one day without the child and wouldn't talk about it. She was living with our mother at the time and all she said was that she had put the baby up for adoption. No-one knew what was going through her mind or why she did it.'

He looked at Laurel as he said sadly, 'It wasn't the same for unmarried mothers then as it is now, was it, Laurel?'

She shook her head, as she said, 'No, there were no pensions or social service groups in those days. You just had to cope any way you could. I guess that was her way.'

Donna had disappeared into a back room while we were talking and came out with some old photo albums to show us.

We all sat close together, gathered around Uncle Terry as he turned the pages.

The handful of photos of our mother and Nanna Mooney that she found did not stir in me the same feelings as my father's photo had, I'm sorry to say. What I did feel was pain: pain at the loss of my mother so early in my life.

In my youth, I'd seen her in my dreams every night. I remembered them so clearly and the feelings of loss that resulted. No matter how fast I ran towards her with my arms out, beseeching her to hold me, the gap never lessened. She always turned and walked away. Why had she given up on me so soon?

Because of her long absences in my youth, my mother was as much a stranger to me as she was to Sandra.

'She wanted to be called Esme,' Uncle Terry said, pulling me out of my reverie as he came across a photo of Mum when she had been his and Aunt Laurel's bridesmaid. 'Our father's name was Esmond and she insisted on being called Esme. She hated the name Merle.' He looked at us and then down at the photos and said, 'You've both got her high cheekbones but apart from that, neither of you look much like her. You look more like your father.' He looked at me and said, 'You've got her eye colour, Patricia.'

Uncle Terry pulled out a photo of Mum holding a cheerful white-haired baby as she smiled into the camera. She looked so happy and I had to bite my lip to stop the tears from coming to my eyes. He turned it over and tried to read the writing on the back that had been faded by age. A hole replaced some of the words, leaving incomplete sentences.

He put his glasses on and said, 'It looks like it says, "This is a good snap of me and the baby only . . .", there's a small hole here but then it says, ". . . for she means the world . . .", there's the hole again and then she says, ". . . not a bad look. What say you? I think she will be tall like you."' He looked over at me. 'I think this is a photo of Esme and you. You can have it if you want it,' he said as he held it out to me.

That had been enough to open the floodgates. I couldn't stop the tears now. I started to cry. What had been the missing words? She'd written, 'for she means the world . . .' I was almost too scared to ask myself the next question. Had the hole replaced the words 'to me' on the back of the photo? *Could this be true?* I cried harder. *Had I meant the world to her? Had she really loved me all along?* All my life I'd desperately wanted her love; wondering why she hadn't loved me and wishing she had, and here she'd written that I'd meant the world to her. I was almost too afraid to believe it but not to believe it would be as painful as losing her all over again. For most of my life, I'd resigned myself to the fact that I hadn't measured up to her expectations. It was a part of my life. I'd accepted it. This photo changed everything. God, how I wanted to believe those words.

I stared at the photo, taking in everything about her. Her hair looked different to how I remembered it. By the time I was six years old she was getting it permed. In this photo, her hair was in a fashionable style I'd seen in old movies. It was still dark but rolled back off her forehead, tucked behind her ears and rolled under to her shoulders.

I felt someone's hands on my shoulders comforting me, but I couldn't take my eyes off the photo.

Uncle Terry was caught up in all the memories now as he continued, 'I remember the first time I met your father.'

I looked up at him as he went on. 'It was my father's funeral and for some reason no women were allowed at the cemetery,' he said. 'Your father turned up to pay his last respects and was asked to leave. I don't remember why. I do remember it was a couple of years before you were born, Patricia. That was in 1952 or 1953. After you were born, he often came with you to visit me at the Post Office in Roma Street where I worked.'

He looked over at Laurel and said, 'We didn't see too much of anybody in those days. I remember the first day I met Laurel. It was at a dance and I walked up to her and asked her to dance. She smiled at me as if she was very happy. We were married three months later.'

They looked at each other and smiled, obviously still in love after all these years.

'We bought a block of land in Garfield Road, Woodridge, and lived in a shed for a while till I built the house we eventually lived in. The children started coming along and then we moved into the house. I felt so proud that I'd built it by myself. It was only small but it was ours. We lived a long way from anyone and to get to work I had to walk quite a long way to catch a train. We didn't have a car and we didn't have a phone. We were pretty much cut off from the family and had no idea of what was happening outside of our little house. We had our hands full, didn't we, Laurel?'

She smiled and nodded. 'And I loved every minute of it.'

'What was Mum like, Uncle Terry?' I asked.

Staring off into the distance while Laurel and our cousins brought us more cups of tea and slices of a homemade cake, he shook his head and said, 'She was a beautiful girl, you know. A little bandy and pigeon-toed, but that was all.'

That was her legacy to me: green eyes and bandy legs.

'She had everything going for her. But she liked lairy things. I suppose the grass was always greener someplace else. I don't think she really knew what she wanted.'

I had the feeling that our mother was on the outer limits of Uncle Terry's ideas of acceptability, that perhaps he was a little ashamed of the mistakes his sister had made all those years ago and was more than willing to put those years behind him.

As we left I hoped that his sister's children had earned his tick of approval.

As much as I'd loved listening to Uncle Terry talking, I was glad to be home. I had so much to think about. My whole outlook had changed. It frightened me that all I could remember were the bad times. I was forty-one now. I didn't want to remember old hurts. But they were always there lately, lurking in the background, ready to spring forward when I least expected it.

I remember reading somewhere years ago that for every happy childhood there are ten unhappy ones. That's what I decided to concentrate on. I was not the only one who had had an unhappy childhood. There were plenty of others who had suffered as well. There would be no self-pity for me.

But why did she give us all up? There had to have been a reason. If she had any dreams, she never mentioned them to me. She wouldn't have, would she? I was only four.

Somewhere through the generations, a thread of weakness had appeared in our family in the form of alcoholism. I knew it then. I know it now. My mother sometimes didn't get up in the mornings after she'd come home stumbling in with and shushing yet another stranger. She'd never even been aware that I'd heard her. The only thing she had been aware of was her body's needs. I hadn't understood then that what she was doing was not natural.

I sometimes think Mum did me a favour. She spared me from continually seeing her unconscious until mid-afternoon. Spared me the sight of seeing her too sick to get up so all she could do was just turn her head to one side and be sick there in her bed. Spared me the embarrassment of seeing her fall over drunk in public. For a child, to see this once would have been enough.

Here was the reason she had sent me away staring me in the face. Mum had done the only thing she could do. She had given me to someone who could raise me and look after me, because she couldn't. Instead, I was left with the memory of a beautiful woman with black hair and green eyes who had written 'for she means the world to me'.

CHAPTER 17

---- ✛ ----

Chook Legs

During the long weekend of Easter, two weeks after meeting Uncle Terry, Sandra and I flew the two hours north to Cairns to visit Annette.

Correspondence between the three of us had progressed with letters and recent photos but there was still tension in the air that morning as Sandra, Farouk and I boarded the plane. David had seen us off at the airport but was on duty over the weekend and so was unable to come with us.

Once on board, I stared out the window while attendants served food and drinks. I wondered if we'd done the right thing. I still wasn't sure.

Cairns, being in the tropics, is almost unbearable in summer and even though it was now autumn, the sun on the day we arrived was still hot enough to melt the tarmac.

Cairns airport was built low but spread out. We walked towards the tunnel that led to the main arrival lounge. Some people were checking bags while others walked straight to the exit doors. This was the time of year when tourists came in their greatest numbers and the place was crowded with people meeting the new arrivals. I noticed advertisements lining the walls and the floor-to-ceiling glass partition, with its white dots at eye level to stop people from walking into the glass door on their way to the carpark. The screens high above our heads announced our flight's arrival.

I scanned the swarming faces, looking for a brunette who could be her. There were dozens of candidates. Tall ones, short ones.

Then I could hear Sandra behind me screaming, 'There she is!'

And she was. Smiling a big, wide smile.

As we walked towards each other, I could feel the emotion swelling up inside me, growing with every step we took. While we all hugged, cried, then laughed, I tried to take in every detail about her.

She was a little shorter than Sandra and me, probably about five-foot two. She was small-boned and dark-haired with green eyes similar in colour to mine, and so petite and beautiful that even I, at 55 kilos, felt like a lumberjack beside her.

Looking at her heart-shaped face, her nose and eyes the same as our mother's, I had no trouble imagining that this was how Mum could have looked at the same age if life had been a little kinder to her.

She introduced us to her husband Don who, surprisingly, was an air traffic controller and had probably talked to David on numerous occasions, neither of them knowing who the other one was. He led us to a van in the parking lot before driving us to their house and introducing us to their four daughters.

Their house was set in a garden with high palms in the front yard and a backdrop of nearby mountains. The humidity hung heavily on us like a wet blanket, making the glasses of chilled wine offered to us in a room adjoining the swimming pool very welcome.

I held up my camera to Don and said, 'Would you take a photo of us?'

That started a flurry of activity as Sandra dug in her purse, saying, 'Oh man, I nearly forgot. Could you take one for me too?' Annette ran to the kitchen and brought hers back to Don as well. We all smiled and held up our wine glasses in a toast to each other. We had so much to talk about but no-one knew where to start.

Each of us was looking at the other two trying to see a resemblance between us all. Sandra looked at her hands and then leant over to see Annette's. She grabbed mine and we all placed our hands on the table.

'I hate my hands,' I said self-consciously. I knew I didn't take enough care of them. They were always in hot, sudsy water and detergent so the skin was shiny and slightly red, and my nails were short and brittle. My knuckles seemed overlarge and veins could be seen close to the surface of the skin. The only saving grace was my long fingers.

All of us looked from one set of hands to the other, comparing size and shape. They were all the same. Almost identical. Mine just looked more used.

I looked up at Sandra and Annette, and noticed their heart-shaped faces looking back at me in surprise. Tears welled up in my eyes as I looked at them.

I could see a resemblance between all of us. I wasn't alone any more. I suppose sisters who grow up together and spend years looking at each other would take this for granted. I knew we never would.

I wondered what it would have been like growing up with them. I was the one in the middle so I would probably always have had one of them to play with. But would Sandra have been the one left out or would Annette, being the eldest, have been the outsider? Did one of them have to be an outsider?

I remembered not so long ago, before all this had happened, I'd been waiting in my doctor's surgery. In a corner sitting together, surrounded by the surgery's toys, were triplets. They were absolutely identical; to me, anyway. Two sat together laughing and showing each other what they had built with their blocks while the other one sat by herself quietly reading, not in the least upset or disturbed about being left out. Was that the way of sisters? Was one invariably left out?

'Take another photo, Don,' I said, looking down again at my hands and placing them beside Sandra's and Annette's.

'Are you going to pay me by the hour or is it going to be a set fee for the weekend?' he laughed as he again shuffled from camera to camera.

I stood up and took my shoes off as I said, 'What about our legs?'

We all stood in a tight circle and raised our skirts a little so that we could see, from above, our legs from the knees down.

'My God,' was all I could say. 'We've all got chook legs!'

We all laughed as we compared our skinny legs.

Sandra said as she looked at me, 'I think yours are the skinniest and bandiest.'

'Maybe so,' I smiled as I looked down at all of our feet, 'but I can tell you both this. I've got the prettiest looking feet out of all of us. Both of you have very ugly feet. Take another photo, Don,' I said.

'Yes, massah,' Don laughed as he bent forward in an exaggerated bow.

The next two days were spent trying to get to know each other and although the expected nervousness was always present, the weekend went quite well considering we were three strangers thrown together so unexpectedly and from such diverse backgrounds.

We walked around the main tourist shopping centre simply talking and learning about each other. We had coffee in little tourist cafés and lunches in restaurants overlooking Cairns harbour. The weather was ideal: hot, sunny days with barely a cloud in the sky and warm nights with light breezes rustling through the palms.

Before we knew it, the weekend was over and we were on our way back to Brisbane.

I walked into my house and felt like I'd never been away.

The television in the family room was blaring while Mark was playing Nintendo on the other television in the lounge room. I could hear music coming from Tony's room and I wondered if 'rap' was supposed to be called music.

'I hope you guys won money on Lotto last night because the next electricity bill is all yours,' I called out as I turned *Oprah* off.

'I'm watching the TV, Mum,' called Tony as he poked his head out of his bedroom door.

'You're watching *Oprah*?' I asked with raised eyebrows.

'Well, I was,' he said half-heartedly.

'Sure you were. Turn it off when you're not watching it.'

I went through each room, collecting the dirty clothes and putting them into the washing machine after separating the whites from the colours. How could two boys wear so many clothes in just two days? Girls I could understand. I had seen Annette's girls change clothes three times a day when I'd been in Cairns, but my boys?

I walked into the kitchen and started taking vegetables out of the fridge to prepare a simple dinner of steak, scalloped potatoes and a green salad, as Tony threw himself into one of the swivel chairs at the kitchen bench.

'How did it go?' he asked.

'Great. Annette looks a little different from Sandra and me

but the similarity is still there. Sort of like you and Mark. Mark is blond and you've got dark hair but you're still clearly brothers,' I tried to explain.

'How could your mum give you up? Do you know why?'

'Nobody will ever know, Tony. It's no use trying to find a solution. There isn't any.'

'I'm never leaving you,' he stated definitely.

'You will,' I said. 'It's the way of things.'

'Nope. I'm going to stay with you always. What would you do with all of your spare time if I left?' he asked innocently.

I thought of the washing in the machine, dinner to prepare, lunches for school tomorrow, the ironing, and the animals to feed, and then I thought of all the things I'd rather be doing.

'Are you really sure you're never leaving?'

'You'd miss me if I went,' he smiled at me confidently.

He was right.

The next day, my papers arrived in the mail, adding nothing startling or new. Annette's papers arrived in the mail the day after mine but with her papers came two bombshells.

We were indeed sisters, but only half-sisters.

The first shock was a comment at the bottom of her letter that read, 'Your birth mother had two daughters born in 1955 and 1959 who were also adopted. Their details are attached. You and your sisters share the same mother but not the same father.'

Her adoption papers stated her father's name as Michael Miller but her birth certificate said 'father unknown'.

'This has been the worst time of my life,' she sobbed over the phone. 'I've got no sense of myself any more. I feel so empty. Two months ago, I knew who I was and who my parents were. Now, everything's changed.'

My mind flashed back to that night when I made the fateful

decision to call her. If I had the time again, would I make that call knowing what I knew now? I'd never meant to hurt anyone. I'd naively thought she would be as happy as I was.

'You're still my sister, Annette. This means nothing to me.'

'Half-sister, Trish. Half-sister. That's all.' I heard the sound of a tissue being pulled out of a box and a sniffle. She continued, 'I'm going to keep looking for my father, though. He'll probably be well into his seventies by now or dead but I have to know. It even comes down to a medical thing. If my doctor asks if there is heart disease or diabetes in my family, I just wouldn't know. I have to try and find him. You understand, don't you?'

'Of course I do.' I had no idea how to comfort her. I always feel awkward around emotion. 'This is something you have to do. I'm so sorry about all of this. I had no idea.'

There was nothing more I could say. I couldn't get the sound of her tears out of my mind.

Then there was the second bombshell.

CHAPTER 18

✤

Bill Bailey Was Here

'We've got a brother too?' Sandra asked, amazed.

She couldn't believe what she had started.

Annette's letter had stated that when I was fourteen (after Dad's death) Mum had been living in Cairns and had signed my adoption papers in the Cairns Department of Children's Services accompanied by a two-year-old boy, who, it turned out, was our half-brother.

His name was William Bailey and he was now twenty-nine years old and living in Townsville. He had been adopted at four years old when our mother died. I hadn't known that Mum had died two years after signing my adoption papers. But then, I didn't know a lot of things.

'Okay. Do you want to start looking for William?' I asked.

'Not me,' said Annette emphatically. 'You go right ahead if you want to. I've got enough things to think about without adding to them.'

It was up to me, so I began looking half-heartedly in the phone book, not expecting to find his name until I thought, *There has to be an easier way of doing this.*

The Salvation Army! The thought came to me like a bolt of lightning. They had people working for them who helped find lost family members every day. I needed to talk to someone who specialised in exactly the sort of situation I had found myself in.

I flicked the pages over until I found the number and wrote it down so that I could ring them first thing in the morning.

At the coffee shop the next morning, Margaret walked in and tossed her bag in the back room then turned to me.

I stood there smiling at her, and she put her hands on her hips and said, 'Out with it. What's happened now?'

'Annette got her papers in the mail yesterday and it says we have a brother, too.'

She stared at me with her eyes wide open and her mouth in the shape of an 'O'. She laughed and shook her head as she said, 'I just love this job. There's always something happening with you. It certainly isn't boring around here. First Sandra, then Annette and now a brother. Where is he and what's his name?'

'His name is William Bailey. Bill Bailey,' I said with a smile as I remembered a song from my childhood. *'Won't you come home, Bill Bailey/Won't you come home,'* I sang and we both laughed.

I had no idea where he was but I was going to find out.

'I have to ring the Salvos to see if they can help me, Margaret. Just call out to me if it gets busy,' I said as I walked into the small office where the phone sat near the deep freezer.

I dialled the number I'd written down and when a soft female voice answered I asked to be connected to a counsellor.

'Can I help you?' a deep, gravelly male voice said after I'd listened to the elevator music for nearly two minutes.

'Yes, I hope so. My sisters and I have just found out that we have a half-brother and I'd like some advice on how to find him.'

'Well, I can give you some ideas if that's what you're after. If you want us to find him for you, you'll have to come in with your birth certificate and the papers from Children's Services as proof of identity. What help would you like?' He sounded very sure of himself—as if he did this every day of his life, which he probably did.

'All I really want is some sort of direction to start in. He's not in the phone book and probably lives in North Queensland. That's where he was born.'

'Okay. There are four places to start looking,' he said. 'The best place to start is the Electoral Office. If he's on the rolls, you'll be able to find his last known address there. If he isn't, then you could try the armed forces. He could be in one of them. They don't have to register for voting. The next place to look would be the police force. Policemen don't have to enrol either, as a matter of security for their personal lives. The last thing I can suggest is he may be in jail. Obviously, they don't have to vote. Have you tried any of these yet?'

'No. You were my first phone call. This isn't going to be easy, is it?' I asked as I looked at the notes that I'd scribbled when he was talking. 'Electoral Office, armed forces, police force or jail. That's it?'

'That's about it. You should find him in one of those. Just call back or come in if you still can't find him but I can't think of anything else that we would do.'

'Thank you. I appreciate your help,' I said.

I hung up and sat back in the chair. The closest Electoral Office was in West End about twenty minutes' drive away, and probably only open between Monday and Friday. The only way that I would be able to get there would be to close the shop early one day and go straight from work. I hated doing that because I knew that at three in the afternoon I would be filthy and smell like the fish I'd been crumbing all day, but I could see no other way.

✦

The next day, I shut the shop doors at 3 p.m., sprayed deodorant all over my clothes and myself, and set off for the Electoral Office. I was lucky enough to find a park between two cars directly outside the office and after three attempts at a reverse park, I finally managed to wedge my Nissan Pulsar between them. And with twenty-five minutes still left in the parking meter. Silently, I said to myself, *Meant to be.*

David often laughed at me when I said things were 'meant to be'. I remember one time we'd been looking through the paper trying to pick a horse for the Melbourne Cup. Almost every person in Australia stops for three minutes on the first Tuesday in November to watch the race after placing a bet. Even people who never place a bet on a horse the rest of the year do so on this day and we were no exception. I had already gone through the list of horses and one name jumped off the page at me.

'Concorde! That's the horse, Dave. That's the one that's going to win!' I'd yelled out to him as he stood in the kitchen making coffee.

'Why on earth would you pick Concorde?' he asked, perplexed. 'It hasn't even been tipped to place.'

'The name, of course. Concorde is French!' I stated. 'It's a sign!'

'Oh, a sign,' he said with a broad smile on his face. 'Let me see if I can guess the logic here. Concorde is French. You're part French. Napoleon is French too. Napoleon is also the name of a cake. People eat cakes in a coffee shop. You own a coffee shop. Oh, my God! A sign! It's meant to be!'

We had both been laughing by the time he'd finished, but I'd still put a bet on it. And lost.

As I walked into the small foyer of the Electoral Office, I noticed it was an historic building dating back to the turn of the century. I found the silence almost overpowering as I tiptoed over to the counter, my steps still echoing loudly on the polished floors.

A sign said 'PLEASE WRITE NAME AND ADDRESS CLEARLY IN REGISTER BOOK'. I pulled it over and did as I was told.

As I finished, a clerk came over and simply said, 'Name?'

'Mine?' I replied in like tone.

'Letter of the alphabet?' she said to me as she looked over the top of her glasses.

'B.' I was getting used to staccato phrases.

She walked away and came back with a tray full of microfilm. She handed them to me and pointed over my shoulder to a desk in the corner where a machine sat waiting for the films.

Obediently, I walked over and sat down.

There were a few William Baileys but none of them had the correct birth date.

One down, three to go, I thought as I stood up and placed the tray back on the counter.

I self-consciously called out, 'Thank you,' as the clerk looked around the partition. I turned around and walked outside to my car. As I opened the door and sat down, I noticed I'd only been inside for ten minutes. It was too late to ring anybody else that day so I pulled out into the busy peak-hour traffic thinking of what I would do the next day.

'I'm not going back to school any more,' Tony informed me as he set the table that night.

'Here it comes,' said Mark.

'And why is that?' I asked.

'On parade today over the loudspeaker, Mr Davies told me to pull my pants up.'

Mark roared with laughter at the memory of it. 'It was really funny, Mum. You're always telling Tony to pull his pants up and not wear them on his hips like a homey. Well, Mr Davies told him to do it in front of the whole school.'

'Shut up, Mark,' yelled Tony.

'Tony, there is no situation that can't be solved with a laugh.' I almost laughed myself. 'Don't take things so seriously. Laugh about it. If you get upset everyone will make fun of you but if you laugh with them, everyone will just forget about it. Besides, I hope the two of you are going to be at school for a lot longer yet. Having an education makes you free, having a career will give you the freedom to do what you want with your lives. I wish I'd stayed at school for a while longer.'

'Didn't you do what you wanted?' Mark asked between gulps of milk.

'Yes, I suppose I did. But I really didn't have much of a choice.'

'Then why do you wish you'd stayed in school?'

'Because then you can do things you want to do, not do them because there's nothing else to do.'

'You didn't stay at school and you're all right. Why do we have to?' asked Tony petulantly.

'Because I don't want the both of you working as hard as I do to make a living.' While I talked, I put parsley around the lamb roast.

'Wouldn't it taste the same without the greenery, Mum?' asked Tony, obviously in a mood.

'Probably. But let's have it looking nice anyway.'

We all sat down and the mood lightened as it normally does when there is food in front of the boys. I poured myself a glass of wine and sat down at the table with them.

Memories of Mum suddenly jumped into my mind as I looked at the glass. The last few weeks had been an eye opener. My parents both drank too much, a slight understatement there. I'd never been a big drinker—I could never afford to be—but I had first-hand knowledge of the consequences of too much drinking. I'd heard it said that if a child has an alcoholic parent, there is a 50 per cent chance that they would be one as well.

What were my chances when both of my parents were heavy drinkers? Was it a genetic thing or was it that the influence of your parents turned you into one? I had no idea.

I decided not to take the chance and mentally limited myself to one glass of wine a night with a meal from then on.

By mid-morning the next day, I'd called directory assistance for the numbers of the navy, army and air force in Canberra. I was passed from department to department in all three but eventually each had the same story. No William Bailey in any of the forces.

Only two choices left, I thought.

Images jumped into my mind of when I worked at Pizza Hut and became friendly with a policeman who had become a regular customer. I hadn't seen him since leaving Pizza Hut years before but maybe he was the one who could help now. I was running out of options. The only choices left were on opposite sides of the law so I said a silent prayer, found the number in the phone book for the police station he worked at, hoping he still did, and dialled the number.

As luck would have it, Damian answered the phone.

'Hello, Damian. It's Trisha, here. I don't know if you remember me or not but years ago I used to work at Wynnum Pizza Hut. Remember?'

'Of course I do. I haven't seen you for ages. What are you doing these days?' he asked jovially.

'I've got my own coffee shop now. No more Pizza Hut for me. Too many hours and too many late nights.'

'Can't stay away from the food business, eh?'

'Ya gots to do what ya gots to do.' I do very bad Jimmy Durante imitations.

He laughed and said, 'What can I do for you?'

'I need your help. Just recently, I found I had this string of family members I never knew about. I've met all of them except for one. A brother. I've tried everywhere to find him. Electoral roll, armed forces and there are only two other places to look. One is to see if maybe he's a policeman and the other is if he's in jail. Hopefully it's the former.'

'I can give you a number to call to see if he's a policeman, that's the best I can do. I'm not supposed to give out any other information.'

'Damian, please, you're my last chance. His name is William Bailey and he could possibly be in Townsville. Can't you just see if he has a record?' I begged.

He hesitated and said, 'I'm taking a big risk doing this. If I get caught, my butt will be on the line.'

I could hear the clicking of keys on the other end of the line and then his voice saying, 'Well, well, well.'

'Have you found something?' I asked, not really wanting to know now.

'Oh, yeah. I found something. Four pages of something.'

I groaned inwardly. 'Okay, you may as well tell me.'

'The first offence was when he was eighteen; just drunk and disorderly. It says here that he was found wandering the streets and they brought him into the watch house. Apparently he said that both his parents had just died and he got a letter in the mail from some government department telling him that he had been adopted. Bad timing, if you ask me.'

All I could see in my mind was the sad image of a forlorn young man feeling abandoned by the world. My heart immediately went out to him.

Damian continued. 'After that, there are a few similar offences. A couple of D & Ds. A couple of driving without a licence while under the influence of alcohol.'

He kept clicking away as he continued. 'Speeding. Nothing serious. Just community service and fines. Not really a criminal.'

Click, click, click. 'Dropped out of sight for a while. No record of anything for a couple of years.'

He laughed and said, 'The last offence was in Ingham six months ago. He must have hitched the 120 kilometres up from Townsville 'cause he sure doesn't have a licence. Anyway, he was brought in drunk after writing graffiti on a park bench. Guess what he wrote.'

'Go ahead. Tell me,' I said, shaking my head.

'He wrote "Bill Bailey was here". Can you believe that?' he laughed. 'In a town of 4000 people, he wrote his name on a park bench. This guy is a classic.'

'Okay, okay. That's my brother you're laughing at, buster.' I was laughing myself. 'Do you have his last address?'

'Sure.' He gave me the address and the name of an officer he knew in Ingham and wished me luck.

Damian was right. Our brother didn't sound like a criminal, just a guy who was handed a raw deal. Innocent and naive, probably. Set adrift at eighteen and lost, but not a criminal.

I tried to imagine what it would have been like for him. Both parents dead by the time he was eighteen and only then finding out that he had been adopted. Totally alone. He must have had so many questions, been so confused. I could only feel sorry for him.

Ingham is a small town of several thousand people in Far North Queensland, Australia's equivalent of the Deep South in America. Ingham sits part way between Cairns (tourism gateway to the Great Barrier Reef) and Townsville, which is a predominantly industry- and military-based city surviving in its dust bowl by damming the Ross River—famous in Australia for its mosquito-borne fever every summer. Ingham survives as a local centre for the sugarcane industry, which is the mainstay of this area.

Directory assistance had no listing for a Bill Bailey in Ingham, so my next phone call had to be to the local policeman who Damian had told me to ring. The chance of this policeman knowing Bill was my last shot.

To my surprise, or maybe it was dismay, he knew Bill, and he was able to lay his hands on Bill's address and phone number with no effort at all. I wasn't sure if that was a good sign or a bad sign. Bill was apparently living with some friends, he said, which was why I had been unable to find his phone listing anywhere.

With Bill now located, I rang Sandra and said, 'We're wasting our talents here. With the way we've both been able to track down our family members, we should start up our own business. "The Looney Mooney Detective Agency". How does that sound?' I laughed.

'Catchy title,' I could hear the smile in her voice, 'but with a name like that, what sort of clients could we expect?'

'Gullible ones? Irish ones? We'd get to put on trench coats and "Jackie O" shades. I've read enough spy novels to make a real go of this.'

'Don't sell the shop just yet, will you?' she replied and we laughed in unison. This sort of banter between us I loved.

I said goodbye and dialled the number. A man answered, 'Hello?' I could hear noises in the background. Voices of children, men, women, loud music, laughter, clinking glasses. I looked at my watch and realised it was 7 p.m. on a Friday night and probably not the best time to call. I'd been caught up in everything and had lost track of the hours.

'Hi,' I said. 'I'm looking for a Bill Bailey. Could you tell me if he lives there?'

'Yeah. Hang on,' he said as he dropped the phone with a clunk. Jimmy Barnes screamed out about cheap wine and a three-day growth, and just as I was thinking of hanging up and calling back the next day, a voice came on the line, slightly slurred but friendly.

'Yeah?'

'Hi. Is this Bill Bailey?' I asked.

'Yeah.' I had a feeling this wasn't going to be easy.

'Bill, you don't know me and I'm not sure if this is the best time for you,' I began. 'Is it all right to talk right now?'

'Yeah.' Not a huge vocabulary either.

I shouted over the music, 'Bill, when I was young I was adopted and about six months ago, a woman contacted me who was also adopted. She found out that we were sisters and that we also have another sister in Cairns and a brother. I hope this is not going to be too big a shock, but it seems that you are our brother.'

I could only hear music and laughter. Nothing else.

'Are you there?' I asked.

'I always wondered if I had a family somewhere,' he started slowly. 'I've been alone for about ten years now but I've always wondered.' It sounded as if he had sobered up instantly.

'Your mother was Merle Rose Mooney, wasn't she?' I asked so that there could be no doubt we shared a mother.

'Yeah. So the letter from the government said. I didn't know I was adopted till I was eighteen. When I was sixteen, my mother died and two years later, my father died. It was a bad time for me. Then the letter arrived.'

I had to strain to hear his voice as it gradually got quieter and quieter.

'You probably won't want to know me. I've been in a little trouble with the law. Don't get me wrong,' he quickly added, 'no robbery or murder or nothing,' he laughed softly, 'but I drink too much, I think. I'm going to stop soon.'

'Bill,' I started, 'we already know about all of that and we still wanted to call you.'

'What are your names?'

'I'm Patricia. Trish. Then there's Annette and Sandra. Annette is the eldest and Sandra is the youngest. You're the youngest now, I guess.' It had just occurred to me.

'Do you remember Mum?' I asked.

'No. The letter said that I was four years old when she died and then I was adopted. I don't remember her at all.'

He had started talking loudly again to be heard over the music, and called out to someone in the background, 'Keep it down!' and the music volume went down a notch.

'I've got a couple of photos of her that I can make copies of,' I said to him. 'Would you like me to send them to you?'

'Yeah. That would be great.' I could hear the wonderment in his voice and I smiled to myself. I knew that feeling well. My life of late was filled with it.

'I'll let you get back to your party. You'll probably get a call from Annette and Sandra sometime soon. They'll want to talk to you as well. Would you like my phone number just in case you want to call me?'

'Well,' he began hesitantly, 'we've got a sort of ban on the phone here. We can get calls but we can't dial out. Saves money, you know?'

'Sure,' I said.

We said our goodbyes and hung up.

'He sounds really nice,' I enthused to each of the girls on separate calls. 'A little innocent but nice.'

Sandra said she would ring him in a few days, but Annette and Don lived only about one and a half hours north of Ingham so they decided they would go and meet him at the weekend.

When Annette called to say she'd met Bill, I could hear a little something in her voice. Something I couldn't quite put my finger on. Something just out of reach. A hesitation.

He had light brown hair, hazel green eyes and a tattoo of a teardrop under one eye, she'd said. And a four-year-old daughter who lived with her half-Aboriginal mother. Thrown in like a 'by the way' was, 'And he looks like Sandra.' Her only comment.

We must have all seemed like a dysfunctional, mismatched bunch to outsiders: Sandra and me with our hang-ups, Bill's wildness and recklessness, and then there was Annette, once confident and sure of herself, now a little lost and bewildered.

She and Sandra barely spoke these days. Problems between them had begun soon after our first visit to Cairns. Sandra couldn't understand why Annette took on the role of the abandoned child, when in actual fact, Sandra and I were the abandoned ones and Annette had had a normal childhood with a loving family.

Sandra wanted a mother more than anything else in the world and here was someone who had a mother but chose to focus on issues that, important as they were to Annette, did not seem so to Sandra. As soon as Annette found out she was adopted, she seemed to have begun to draw away from the thing she had that Sandra had always craved: a mother. Sandra had little time for Annette's roller-coaster moods and her visits to a counsellor for depression and lethargy.

Even though I had some similar feelings to Sandra's, I knew it had been a shock to Annette to find she had been adopted at birth and I was prepared to try to work through it all. Sandra, though, took her pain and began to withdraw from Annette and a little from me.

CHAPTER 19

✛

The Other Half

Christmas came and went.

Don had accepted a job transfer to Brisbane, and he and Annette were in the process of finding a school for Mary and a house for them all to live in. All the girls were protesting at the upheaval. The reasons given to them for the move were that Annette's parents were old now and unwell, but we all knew that the main reason for it was so she could be near her sisters.

But things didn't turn out quite as she'd expected. On top of her and Sandra only speaking now and again, Annette's father died before she left Cairns. Everything, plus the move to Brisbane, almost unbalanced her. There was just too much for her to take in all at once.

Two weeks before Christmas, Bill and his little daughter, Josie, came down for a visit. They stayed with David and me during the Christmas break, and Bill tried so hard to make a good impression by barely drinking at all.

We took them to see different parts of Brisbane when we could, but it wasn't easy with both David and me still working for the first two of those three weeks. Qantas rostered all their pilots a month in advance so there had been no opportunity for David to ask for any extra time off. As for me, I only had one week a year off and that was between Christmas and New Year. Joining up all the public holidays during that time gave me about eight days. It was better than nothing.

We drove Bill and Josie down to the beach at Burleigh Heads on the Gold Coast for one day and into the 'Coast Hinterland' another day. 'Natural Arch' has always been a favourite of mine and if it wasn't almost a two-hour drive away, I'm sure we would go more often. I love the coolness of the rainforest, and the taste and smell of the fresh waterfalls that fill small swimming holes to the brim. Josie was amazed at the lizards, birds and bush fowl that came up to her for left-over food, eating right out of her hand.

Summer had seemed hotter and stickier than I remembered from previous years. Long drives to the coast were abandoned and South Bank became the alternative. We packed picnic lunches, swimsuits and towels and headed into South Brisbane. South Bank is a hugely successful development that once used to be an industrial area on the opposite side of the river from the city centre. It had always been an eyesore until Brisbane hosted Expo '88 and it had been turned into a huge complex with artificial beaches full of beautiful white sand, tourist shopping areas and scores of cafés, restaurants and little kiosks dotted over the three acres. An artificial rainforest with several rock pools overlook the river where a stage has been erected for evening concerts and New Year's Eve celebrations.

At the Christmas party, our last get-together for everyone, I could see reality setting in for Bill. He knew he had to go back.

A week after Christmas, they went home reluctantly. Bill was like a little boy being sent back to boarding school after a holiday. But he had his job, his girlfriend Daisy and her small brood of two to return to.

His life, everything, was in Far North Queensland. I can see him always living there. Farming and fruit picking is the only life he knows. The big cities would eat him alive. He's a simple man with simple tastes.

Recently, he rang to tell me that he'd won third prize in a gardening competition in Bowen. My brother? Gardening?

'I didn't know you were a gardener, Bill.'

'I'm not,' he said. 'I just do what Daisy tells me to do.'

Thinking of my family at Christmas reminded me that I still hadn't ordered my own birth certificate. I'd seen Sandra's and Annette's, and had copies of them tucked away in a special folder along with Dad's death certificate, my adoption papers, photos and the letter from the State Children's Department. All catalogued and at my fingertips when needed. But I didn't have my own birth certificate.

David drove me to the Registry Office to order it and I paid the extra fee to have it ready in only two hours instead of the usual twenty-four. Once I set my mind to something, nothing short of an earthquake can budge me from doing it. I had to have my certificate and I had to have it now.

Back home, we sat at the breakfast bar while I smiled at the certificate with my parents' names next to mine. I waver between being French and Irish depending on the situation but, in reality, I am immensely proud of my mixed heritage. I'm neither one nor the other. I'm both.

I glanced at the box marked 'siblings'.

I knew I wouldn't find Annette's name there as she had been adopted at birth and therefore not regarded as my sibling. I also understood that I was listed on Sandra's because I hadn't been adopted until much later and we were sisters until her adoption at almost four months old. But on mine, while the 'living' section was empty, the deceased section contained two words that jumped out at me . . . 'one female'!

'Dave! What's this?' I asked as I pointed to the words.

'Trish, it's probably just a typing mistake.' He had been my rock over the past year but I think he was hoping there weren't any more of us.

But this was an inconsistency. There were no deceased children as far as we all knew. We each had our papers and there had been no mention of a death in any of them.

I couldn't let this go. Somewhere on either side was a stubbornness gene and I had a full quota. I had to find out. The puzzle was not completed yet.

By 8.30 a.m. the next day, I was parking my car near the Registry Office. The January sky was bright and blue, and the city rumbled with life. A heat haze was already rising from passing cars. The morning sun warmed my shoulders as I walked up to the office.

I walked through a door with gold lettering announcing 'Registry Office' and let my eyes adjust to the dimness after the brightness of Brisbane's sun.

It had the glum atmosphere of a government department. I glanced around, looking for the clerk who had helped Sandra when she'd come in on previous occasions. 'A slight man. Short,' she'd said.

There was only one man out of the four clerks. Through experience, I've learnt that 'you catch more flies with honey than with vinegar', so I walked over to him with a bright smile on my face, and tried to look amiable and ignorant. It didn't take much effort—I had no idea what to expect. I asked him if he could help me with the problem I had and showed him the certificate.

'I remember your sister coming in here,' he smiled. 'So she found you, eh? Good for her.'

'Can you help me? I'm not sure where to go from here.'

He looked over his shoulder and whispered, 'Wait a minute.'

It looked like I wouldn't have to go through the 'pay now, come back tomorrow' routine that was normal for this department. After only ten minutes he returned and said, 'Yep, this is right. There was a deceased female and she was one of a set of twin girls.'

The twins! Paula was right! I almost cheered. 'If there were twins,' I said thoughtfully, 'and one died, then there's one still alive. Right?'

He nodded.

'So, my next question is, how do I find her?'

He looked at me and shook his head, as he said slowly, 'No, you've misunderstood me. There were twins, and one did die, but you were the other twin.'

I must have stood with my mouth open for quite a while, not quite able to comprehend what he had said. I stuttered out, 'But searches have been done and nothing about twins has turned up. Why?'

'Your twin was stillborn,' he said. 'In those days, birth certificates were only issued to living children. If she had lived for even a minute,' he went on to explain, 'she would have been registered with a birth and death certificate but, as such, there were no certificates issued.'

I thanked him and walked out in a daze. On that hot summer morning, people still walked to work, still shopped, and still stopped their cars at stoplights. Life continued around me. I saw none of it. I wandered for a couple of hours, oblivious, before I came to a park bench and sat down. I must have sat there for an hour just staring at the ground.

I knew I had to call Blackall Hospital, where I was born, to make sure that everything the clerk had said was the truth.

✠

Paula had told me that Dad had spent a lot of time in Central Queensland in the post-war years, getting out in the fresh, clean country air to help his ongoing chest troubles.

Blackall is in Central Queensland—a mainly pastoral region which is made up of fairly small properties that are passed down through generations of farming folk. Dad took the opportunity to obtain casual work around these properties transporting stock and produce. I was born in Blackall, the only township in this region that could boast a hospital.

Knowing all about the delays that I could expect from hospital records sections, I expected a long wait for my records.

A bright, cheery female answered the phone at the hospital, and when I asked to be put through to the person who handled archived files, she said, 'That's me. I also handle admissions, discharges, and a few other jobs. I just put a different hat on,' she laughed. She told me that in the twelve years she had been there, only a dozen babies had been born. Blackall was not a big town. My records would not be hard to find, apparently. The ease and speed of everything was astounding.

Barely five minutes later, she was back with my records.

'I've got them,' she said. 'Let me see.' I could hear pages being turned and then, 'Yep, that information is correct. It says here that your mother, Merle Rose Mooney, gave the father's name as Ernest Joseph Gourgaud. She gave birth to twin girls but only one survived. I'm sorry, but no cause of death has been written in the file. It just says that the surviving twin girl was 5 pounds 13 ounces and named Patricia Therese, while the stillborn girl was only 4 pounds 12 ounces.'

No doubt about it then.

How did I feel? I had no idea. How can you miss something you've never had? But I did. I felt numb. Sad, with a heavy feeling of loss.

'There is one more piece of information that I'm not sure you're aware of,' she continued. 'It says that during routine tests, a small spot of tuberculosis was discovered on the lung of the surviving twin. Future and frequent X-rays was the recommendation by the attending medical staff.'

Another piece of the puzzle had fallen into place. I'd never had any problems with my lungs in my youth, but I remembered the chest X-rays I'd had with Dad at Greenslopes Hospital.

Those many visits had been to keep an eye on any developments in my own lungs.

CHAPTER 20

A Black Velvet Band

That's it. No more. I thought. I was sure I'd come to the end of my search. I'd reached saturation point and I resolutely decided to start concentrating on the future and not the past. I wanted no more surprises.

It was now January and all of this had happened since last February. So much in only eleven months.

Recently, I've wondered why things developed so fast after that first phone call from Sandra. At the risk of sounding whimsical, I can feel the presence of my father every day, guiding and helping me, and sometimes simply being near. The only way I can reconcile this with what I have been taught in Catholic institutions and what I believe now, is that my father has spent his time in 'Purgatory' doing his penance and is now actively redeeming his errors in life by enhancing mine. This is only wishful thinking on my part, I know, but it sits well with my Celtic origins. I believe he has given to me what I've always wished for and what he could never attain—a complete family. Maybe even Mum has been watching out for me.

After Sandra, Paula, Annette, Bill, my twin, Uncle Terry, cousins, etc., etc., etc. . . . . I was just about to overdose on relatives, so with a silent prayer of thanks to Dad I added a PS:

You can stop now.

There will always be doubts and unanswered questions about what happened all those years ago, but some things are best left as they are, since the people who could tell us the story have long since been buried themselves. All we can do is try to join the little pieces that we have together as best we can, be satisfied with what we do know, and then get on with our lives.

In my heart, I feel I shouldn't judge my parents without knowing the full circumstances. I should simply trust that they did the best they could and made their decisions in the hope that they were the right ones.

Friends and family would probably have influenced them a great deal, and shame was probably uppermost in their minds. I have little comprehension of the times my parents lived in. They would have relied on their family for help, and if no offer came from them and with no government assistance available at the time, adoption or institutions were the only alternatives.

I do know that Mum had wanted both of the baby girls she had adopted out. The hospital records show the comments, 'This baby is not for adoption,' but in both cases, within four months, they had been given up with no explanation.

My heart swells with happiness now, knowing that I experienced my father's love, even my mother's in a strange sort of way, and I thank them every day for the choices they did make. I hate to think of where my sisters and I would be now if we had all been kept.

It's three and a half years on now and the four of us are still struggling with all we have learnt.

It was over the first year or so that phone calls between Sandra and Annette became rare, something Annette could not understand. 'After all, Sandra started this,' she said. They never speak at all now. Annette finds it hard to recognise Sandra's pain when her own seems so overwhelming.

Also, she can't understand why Sandra held back part of herself in the early meetings when this was a time for each to be learning about the other.

I've tried explaining to Annette that time and patience were all Sandra needed. Just for Annette and me to be there whenever she needed us, with no reproaches on the length of time between calls.

'Call her and talk about everything and anything. That's what I do. Don't wait for Sandra to call you.' I tried to make Annette see that establishing a sibling relationship was as big a step for Sandra as it was for her and that everyone reacts differently to situations.

This patience with Sandra has paid off for me. Sandra and I are as close as sisters could be. Closer.

I remember the exact day when Sandra's and my relationship became solid. It had been my forty-second birthday. David had refused to tell me where we were going. 'Dress up,' was all he said. We drove towards the city but kept going along Coronation Drive towards Mount Coot-tha. Every young couple in Brisbane has been to Mount Coot-tha at some time or other. The lookout from the top is spectacular, especially on a clear night when the glittering lights of Brisbane can be seen distinctly. As we approached the turn-off for Mount Coot-tha, I exclaimed, 'The Lookout Restaurant—how wonderful!' But as the summit came into view, David slowed down and did a U-turn, then stopped on the downgrade so that we could look at the lights. We stepped out of the car and leant back on the bonnet. While cars passed and horns honked, he knelt down, held an engagement ring up to me and proposed. It was the sort of magical moment every woman dreams of and I took no time to accept.

We drove into the city, parked and started walking. I was on Cloud Nine. I still had no idea where we were going and I really didn't care. I was with the man I loved and we would soon be married.

'How about a drink at Gilhooley's first?' Dave said. 'We've got time.'

We'd been to Gilhooley's a couple of times before and it was turning into our favourite haunt. It was always busy, always noisy and very Irish.

It was only 7.30 p.m. but the place was packed with people and we had to push our way through the crowds. Every seat was taken and the air was so thick with smoke, you could cut it with a knife. *I'll probably be deaf after tonight*, was my first thought.

We passed booths filled with people eating and drinking and to my right, I could see the band. One woman played a fiddle, one a penny whistle, while two men played mandolins.

'There's a band on tonight,' I turned and yelled at Dave.

'That's not all that's here tonight,' he yelled back over the din, smiling and pointing his finger.

Tables were set up around the dance floor, and around one large table I saw Sandra, Farouk, Donna, Paula and Barry smiling at me.

Tears came easily as I hugged Dave then kissed and laughed with everyone else. I knew I would never forget this night as long as I lived. Donna said that Annette couldn't make it, and I knew the tension between Sandra and Annette had been a factor. But tonight I wouldn't think about it.

After our meals, Paula, Barry and Donna said their goodbyes and left the rest of us to sit and listen to the band. They were in full swing by now and the noise level had risen even more. The lead singer started singing 'The Wild Colonial Boy', and everyone started clapping and singing along.

David and Farouk were trying to talk to each other, their words lost in the noise; Sandra watched the band and I looked around. Old books lined the walls on picture rails and a map of Ireland hung on another wall showing the location of all the different clans. Every Irish pub I'd been in had a map like that hanging somewhere. I strained to see where 'Mooney' originated but couldn't see through the crowds and the smoke haze. On another far wall, pictures of people from the 1800s dressed in their best clothes and looking grim and uncomfortable, were scattered around.

I glanced back at the band. A few couples were dancing. The women were jigging and the men were shuffling their feet and hopping from one foot to the other. Everyone was laughing and clapping.

The band started playing a song about a woman wearing a black velvet band, and simultaneously Sandra and I started singing along. David and Farouk both stared at us. 'How do you know all the words?' David mouthed at me. I shrugged but kept singing.

Sandra leant over and yelled, 'At the home . . . Sister Philomena . . .' I couldn't hear the rest of what she said.

A roar of applause was followed by a fast tune that set our feet tapping. 'Let's dance,' I yelled to Sandra.

She nodded and we fought our way through the mass of bodies.

There we were. Both jigging as we'd been taught so long ago—hands clenched by our sides and lifting our legs high, our backs ramrod straight. Identical steps. Identical moves. We'd learnt to do this so long ago but everything came back so clearly. I could still see Sister Philomena's smiling face as she spun around with her habit flapping. I understood the happiness she felt.

We fought our way back to the table, both laughing and puffing at the same time. Farouk held up a wine glass and two fingers to a waitress, and she disappeared into the crowd.

We both picked up our purses and made our way to a door marked '*Mna*' and walked in. The sound was magically cut off as the door closed.

Sandra looked at me and I could see the emotion in her eyes.

'Please be patient with me. I look at you and I can't believe you're actually my sister. I've never felt like this before.' She wiped the tears from her eyes.

'After forty-two years without you, I'd wait forever,' I said. 'I love you.'

Annette and I, too, disagree about a lot of things. I think I disappoint her a little. She once said to me, 'Why can't you just empathise with me? Why must you try to solve my problems? Why can't you be more like my friends and just show me sympathy? They know what to do.'

I'd been very hurt by her outburst. Her way was not mine. I can see no use in sitting by and feeling sorry for her. My way is to find solutions. What about trying this? What about trying that? I'd tried to explain my reasoning to her. 'It's like you're in quicksand, Annette, and all of your friends are standing around watching you sink but only saying, "Poor Annette, I feel so sorry for you." What good is that? You'll still sink. I'm the only one with my hand out to you trying to pull you out. But you have to reach out to me, too. You have to come halfway to me.'

But she feels that her life has been turned upside down and she is still trying to come to terms with the feeling that her life has been a complete lie. She still doesn't know who her father is and her birth mother was an alcoholic, unlike the solid, stable mother she had known all her life.

I've tried to convince her that she was the luckiest of us all and should be grateful to the Miners for all they've done for her, but she is only now coming to terms with everything that has happened, and the fact that she is still the same person she was almost four years ago. A certain amount of acceptance has replaced her frantic search for a name to put on her birth certificate.

Sandra's pain comes from the rejection in her life.

As I did, she left home as a rebellious sixteen year old to make a life of her own, having never really gotten over the hurt and rejection of her early years in Nazareth, making wrong decisions and jumping in at the deep end when choices had to be made.

For her, the experience as a preschooler of being rejected in the choice between herself and her adopted sister Jill, was devastating. To find that I had been brought back out of the home while she, as a baby, had been given away for adoption added to her feelings of rejection and was almost more than she could bear.

Like me, she finds it difficult to trust people, and is very wary. She has a quick sense of humour, a sparkling wit, but not wanting to be hurt again, will not let anyone close to her until she feels she can trust them. I can certainly understand and relate to this, since our early years are so very similar. From experience, I have learnt that trust is earned and only comes with time.

The misunderstandings and hurts are still raw and these hurdles prevent reconciliation between Annette and Sandra. Given time I hope this will change. It pains me to see them both hurting like this but we all have our ghosts to exorcise. I, too, have pain to overcome.

At times, the memory of that little seven-year-old girl, with her own feelings, memories and personality, abandoned without a second thought, is more painful than the physical beatings I endured. I had felt that Mum didn't love me enough even to visit me once in the home. My childhood still haunts me.

But one thing I have learnt is that my past has made me the

person I am today. That's the process of life. I now feel strong in myself. I know it really wasn't me my mother was giving up; it was the life she had made for herself and the mistakes she'd made that she wanted to be rid of.

I am at peace with that.

Through all the hardships over the past few years, I've come to know just how much I love my sisters and how lonely my life once was before they changed it. I'm so proud to have them.

In a way, I've reached my own Nirvana.

CHAPTER 21

✢

Seizing the Day

Through all of this, there were two things that I felt I still had to do. The first was to visit Dad's grave.

With explicit directions from Paula, I found it at the far end of a rather neglected part of Nudgee cemetery where some graves had clearly not been visited in many years and others had only a bare wooden cross to indicate there was even a gravesite present. Most of the headstones were concrete and sterile-looking, while the grass that surrounded them had long since been mowed.

The afternoon sun cast long shadows around me as I sat cross-legged on the grass. Tears came easily as I touched his head-stone, so hard, cold and barren. I so wished that things had been different; for Mum and Dad, for all of us. I wished that their dream of a happy future had been fulfilled. What would have started as a bright new life had soon turned into something else: a hopeless situation. The run-down flat would soon have lost its charm as the relationship deteriorated.

I'd been back to Boundary Street: back to my roots. Everything had changed. Gone were the squalid flats and in their place were bright modern ones. Gone were the small shops, the electrical store, newsagent and bakery. All replaced with more flats. No trace of my childhood remained except for the Alliance Hotel.

David took me there for a drink one hot day when I was feeling morbid. I'd sat in the same spot that I had when I was barely five and Dad and Larry had drunk and talked quietly. Why did I have the urgent need to do this?

I took David to Rose Street and there was Nanna Mooney's old house. Gone were the fishbone-ferns outside the white picket fence. The hot sun beat down on a fresh coat of paint.

The past was gone. Replaced and forgotten. It occurred to me that I should do the same. Forget the past. Put it behind me and look to my future, full of hope and promise.

Turn the page.

As I sat on the grass near Dad's grave, I still longed for that one last visit that he had asked for; longed to hear his voice just one more time. I felt as vulnerable as the seven year old who held him tight begging him not to leave. The feeling was so intense, I could almost smell the smoke that was always present on his clothes. His visits had given me hope, a feeling that I was worth something to somebody. Without those visits, I simply would have given up.

There was one thing left to do . . . go back to Nazareth House.

'Trisha was like a little girl being told she had to go to the dentist,' I heard David telling Sandra. 'Even after she'd decided she had to go back, it took weeks to try and turn the plan into an event. It seemed as though there was always an excuse as to why we didn't have time to drive the twenty minutes over there. I still remember as we finally came around the corner and the beautiful old convent building appeared,' Sandra pulled a face at the word 'beautiful' but let him continue, 'Trish started physically curling up in the car seat. I could see her hands clenching tight into fists and her knees pulling up towards her chest. As we turned into the long palm-lined driveway, she started looking around like a frightened animal. I must admit that even I was starting to worry, after telling her so confidently that it was just a building. She started talking softly as we slowly drove towards it. "That gate was where we saw the black dog . . . We used to run amongst the cowpats over there . . . the gargoyles are gone . . . there's the statue of Mary . . . I hated that front door . . . that's the nuns' quarters." As we drove around the back of the building, her apprehensiveness lessened slightly as the renovated grounds became less familiar. There were car parks and new sections of the buildings that weren't there thirty years ago. While the unfamiliarity seemed to make her slightly more comfortable, as I went around to open her door I heard her mumbling that she wasn't sure she could do this. My heart was starting to ache. I could see how much distress she was in, but I also knew that this had to be done, so I took her hand firmly and assured her I'd never let go and wouldn't leave her there. The main entrance is now at the rear of the building with modern automatic glass doors. From there on we had some great luck . . .'

. . . If I'd had to go by myself, I would have turned around at that point and sped away without going in. I kid myself that I'm strong, but I couldn't have done it alone. With my hand firmly in his, David led me across the new car park and along the now-carpeted corridor that had once been cold marble.

Two nuns were walking down the corridor and passed us

with a smile and a nod. They still wore their traditional habits with only their faces showing and I almost smiled as I remembered the description from the movie *The Blues Brothers*. Penguins, they'd called the nuns. Nowadays, most orders wear normal clothes. Well, not really normal as such. They don't wear miniskirts, pumps and boob tubes, and you don't see nuns shopping at Dotti. The severe habits showed how strict this order was. I could certainly vouch for that from experience.

It turned out that the room labelled 'Reception' was once the office where I sat like a street urchin, swinging my legs on my first day. A feeling of familiarity washed over me.

We walked into the office and behind the reception desk sat Michelle Dwyer, someone I'd played tennis with when my boys were little but lost touch with after my divorce from Rob.

'Michelle Dwyer?' I asked. 'Is that you?'

'Trish? Wow, how long has it been?' She stood up and walked over to us.

'Too long,' I replied. I hugged her, then introduced her to David and explained to her why we were there. Some of my trepidation had disappeared with the sight of her. I had another ally.

'Is Sister Philomena still here?' I asked with apprehension in my voice. I expected to hear the clack of her beads at any moment, dreading the noise yet strangely wanting to hear it just the same. In my mind, she was still the robust nun who almost marched down the corridors. I had forgotten that thirty years had passed. I felt like that little girl again, waiting for her to turn the corner.

'No,' Michelle replied. 'Sister Philomena died about five years ago. She was sick for a long time. You'd probably remember Mary Kinnane, though. I'd say she was here when you were. She works here now. I'll see if she's around.'

Then in walked Mary Kinnane, or Mary Williamson, as I knew her: the girl who 'confessed' to car-stealing and smoking so many years ago. Life never ceases to amaze me.

She laughingly called herself the GDB (General Dogs Body) and with one arm draped casually over my shoulders, she explained to me that Nazareth hadn't been an orphanage since 1982. It was now solely a home for the aged.

The changes were confusing after all those years.

The dining room and all the dormitories were now sectioned off into separate units, but my memory of up to fifty beds in my dormitory could not have been correct. Only a dozen units filled the entire space and the enormous bathroom that had seemed so cavernous was now only a storage room for the cleaners to use.

When we stepped into St Bernard's Hall, I looked around in amazement. I remembered it as being a huge room with what seemed like a hundred children either sitting or milling around. In actual fact, it could only hold forty people at a pinch. How had they all fitted in it? I had trouble believing it was the same room!

'It's been cut in half!' I mumbled.

Mary shook her head and smiled.

As I looked around, I noticed that the windows were the original ones with the same brick border I remembered so well. The French doors that led out to the verandah overlooking the driveway and on to the ocean were still the same. The room that ran along the auditorium where the dentist had seen us was the same. But everything was so very much smaller.

Memories started flooding back.

. . . Sister Philomena directing us to have all the chairs lined up in perfectly straight lines for when relatives came to sit and watch us singing and dancing at Christmas . . .

. . . performing our own version of 'Swan Lake' as we tried to stand on our toes while pirouetting clumsily in our ballet outfits, our arms above our heads with fingertips touching in the classic 'Swan Dance', and every bit as graceful as baby elephants . . .

. . . the monthly Sunday movies when we were packed so tightly we could feel the other kids around us breathing as we all sat watching the screen and eating the lollies we had bought down at the shopping centre.

The tour continued to the classroom, now a bright, cheery sunroom, not the gloomy room cluttered with desks that I could still see in my mind. Backtracking down the corridor and passing through what was now the cleaners' room, we walked on through my old locker room, now another bright sunroom overlooking a courtyard.

This courtyard was once the concrete playground where I had spent so many hours. I'd sat there on my first day and once a month I'd waited there for Dad to arrive. I'd skipped rope and danced jigs there. It was unrecognisable. It was now a compact garden with seats scattered around and flowers swaying in the breeze.

Everything was so peaceful.

I remembered walking the interminable distance every morning from my dormitory to the dormitory assigned to the little ones. Incredibly, they were each on opposite sides of this small garden, only a short walk across from one to the other. Barely a one-minute walk!

The chapel where I had stood shivering from the cold those many mornings in winter now had carpeting and padding for the knees. It still smelt of incense and candle wax. Light filtered through the stained glass behind the altar, giving it a softness that I hadn't noticed when I was a child.

The corridor that led to the chapel from my dormitory had seemed to go on for miles to my tiny young legs, but was only a matter of about fifty metres from one end to the other.

I gaped at everything in disbelief. The doorways weren't as big and the windows weren't as dark, and as I stood staring, I felt like I had come to the wrong orphanage.

Everything was familiar but not quite the same. As I looked around, it suddenly occurred to me that the problems and hurts, so huge at the time, had grown as I grew until they were all out of proportion.

There were no demons in the rafters or devils in the hallways.

It was, after all, just a building!

The relief was staggering and immediate. I felt as though a huge weight had been lifted off my shoulders as the tears came to my eyes yet again. It was as if I had suddenly stepped out of the darkness of a cave and into the sunlight, feeling the warmth of the sun on my face for the first time in thirty years.

According to Mary, over the years other girls I remembered had also returned, with much the same result. Monica. Christine. Freda. It had even taken Mary's husband three attempts before he convinced her to step back through those doors again and face her past.

It's said that we all have our own private demons which torment us. We all have to fight them and even though we may not come out unscathed, we hope to come out stronger for the battle and with a certain degree of confidence.

I myself have had days when I've tried to remember the cooling breezes in summer on the hill, the birds chirping in the trees at dawn, the smell of the salt spray from the ocean below. Days when I've tried to think of any memory that didn't hurt, but couldn't find one. But now, I look back without the fear and bitterness that once almost consumed me. I've come to realise that no-one can change what happened, because the past is just that—past.

Because of that, I am not the frightened child I was any more, filled with a need to please and to be accepted. I have lost most of my shyness and timidity, and I am very different from the girl who saw her life spread before her in hopelessness and pain. These days, people too readily discount human resilience, believing they are compelled to react to external forces that are beyond their control.

I'd tried filling the gaps in my life, reliving the uncertainty and pain, and discovering that filling in all those gaps doesn't necessarily make everything right, but that it helps me to cope with what I do know. The picture may not be whole but at least it's recognisable.

As a fanciful child, I had always dreamt of a perfect world, but now, as an adult, I know there is no such thing. And neither are the people in it. All of us are simply striving to do the best we can with the hand we've been dealt. I've come to realise that it's not only choosing the right path that counts, it's the journey as well—what we learn and how we use that knowledge.

I've heard it said that people are lonely because they build walls not bridges, and I guess I believe that. More and more I find we are never given anything in life that we can't handle and the difficulties we experience are meant to make us better people, not bitter people.

I've been able to clarify everything and put it all into perspective. I've been able to rid myself of the anger and bitterness that I kept within me so long and I've come to realise that there is no point in being angry any more.

At forty-five, I feel fulfilled and whole, rejoicing in the things that most people take for granted. I have more assorted relatives than I could ever have imagined and a future filled with people I have come to love and who love me.

These days, I try to spend more time with my family and friends and less time worrying about non-essential things. Whenever possible, life should be savoured, not endured. I'm trying to recognise these moments as they happen now and cherish them. 'Some day' and 'one of these days' have gone from my vocabulary. I try to keep in touch with family members and close friends as much as possible. It's those little things left undone that annoy me now—if I put off seeing good friends I've been meaning to get in touch with—someday. Or if I don't tell my husband and my children how much I truly love them.

I'm trying not to put off, hold back or save anything any more. When I open my eyes every morning, I tell myself that this day is special. I'm living every day now as if it were my last, enjoying what I have missed all my life up until now.

It seems like such a long journey in such a short time from the loneliness that was my world.

Carpe diem! (Sister St Jude would be proud of me.)